ABOUT THIS PUBLICATION

FOR SERVICE ASSISTANCE

Customer Service Department
704.898.0770

North Carolina General Statues is published by The Muliti-Media Group of Greater Charlotte in Charlotte, North Carolina. Copyright 2015 by the Multi-Media Group of Greater Charlotte. This book or parts thereof may not be reproduced in any form, stored in a retrieval system, or transmitted in any form by any means—electronic, mechanical, photocopy, recording or otherwise—without prior written permission of the publisher, except as provided by United States of America copyright law.

The records required by U.S. Code 2257(a) through (c) and the pertinent regulations 28 C.F.R. Cli. 1, Part 75 with respect to this publication and all materials associated with such records are maintained by The Multi-Media Group of Greater Charlotte, Publisher and available for review by Attorney General.

www.visionbooks.org

Copyright © 2015 by MMGGC
All rights reserved!

TID: 5031711
ISBN (10) digit: 150259854X
ISBN (13) digit: 978-1502598547

123-4-56789-01234-Paperback
123-4-56789-01234-Hardback

First Edition

090520140547

Printed in the United States of America

2015 EDITION

North Carolina Criminal Law And Procedure-Pamphlet # 21

Printed In conjunction with the Administration of the Courts

North Carolina Criminal Law and Procedure
Pamphlet Reference Guide

Chapters	Pamphlet
Chapter 1 Civil Procedure	1
Chapter 1 Civil Procedure (Continue)	2
Chapter 1A Rules of Civil Procedure	2
Chapter 1B Contribution.	2
Chapter 1C Enforcement of Judgments.	2
Chapter 1D Punitive Damages.	2
Chapter 1E Eastern Band of Cherokee Indians.	2
Chapter 1F North Carolina Uniform Interstate Depositions and Discovery Act.	2
Chapter 2 - Clerk of Superior Court [Repealed and Transferred.]	3
Chapter 3 - Commissioners of Affidavits and Deeds [Repealed.]	3
Chapter 4 - Common Law	3
Chapter 5 - Contempt [Repealed.]	3
Chapter 5A - Contempt	3
Chapter 6 - Liability for Court Costs	3
Chapter 7 - Courts [Repealed and Transferred.]	3
Chapter 7A – Judicial Department	3
Chapter 7A – Continuation (Judicial Department)	4
Chapter 7A – Continuation (Judicial Department)	5
Chapter 7B - Juvenile Code	5
Chapter 8 - Evidence	6
Chapter 8A - Interpreters for Deaf Persons [Recodified.]	6
Chapter 8B - Interpreters for Deaf Persons	6
Chapter 8C - Evidence Code	6
Chapter 9 - Jurors	6
Chapter 10 - Notaries [Repealed.]	6
Chapter 10A - Notaries [Recodified.]	6
Chapter 10B - Notaries	6
Chapter 11 - Oaths	6
Chapter 12 - Statutory Construction	6
Chapter 13 - Citizenship Restored	6
Chapter 14 - Criminal Law	7
Chapter 14 –Criminal Law (Continuation)	8
Chapter 15 - Criminal Procedure	9
Chapter 15A - Criminal Procedure Act (Continuation)	10
Chapter 15A - Criminal Procedure Act (Continuation)	11
Chapter 15B - Victims Compensation	11
Chapter 15C - Address Confidentiality Program	11
Chapter 16 - Gaming Contracts and Futures	11
Chapter 17 - Habeas Corpus	11

Chapter 17A - Law-Enforcement Officers [Recodified.]	11
Chapter 17B - North Carolina Criminal Justice Education and Training System [Recodified.] Chapter 17C - North Carolina Criminal Justice Education and Training Standards Commission	11
	11
Chapter 17D - North Carolina Justice Academy	11
Chapter 17E - North Carolina Sheriffs' Education and Training Standards Commission	11
Chapter 18 - Regulation of Intoxicating Liquors [Repealed.]	12
Chapter 18A - Regulation of Intoxicating Liquors [Repealed.]	12
Chapter 18B - Regulation of Alcoholic Beverages	12
Chapter 18C - North Carolina State Lottery	12
Chapter 19 - Offenses against Public Morals	12
Chapter 19A - Protection of Animals	12
Chapter 20 - Motor Vehicles	13
Chapter 20 - Motor Vehicles (Continuation)	14
Chapter 20 - Motor Vehicles (Continuation)	15
Chapter 20 - Motor Vehicles (Continuation)	16
Chapter 21 - Bills of Lading	17
Chapter 22 - Contracts Requiring Writing	17
Chapter 22A - Signatures	17
Chapter 22B - Contracts Against Public Policy	17
Chapter 22C - Payments to Subcontractors	17
Chapter 23 - Debtor and Creditor	17
Chapter 24 – Interest	17
Chapter 25 – Uniform Commercial Code	18
Chapter 25 – Uniform Commercial Code (Continuation)	19
Chapter 25A – Retail Installment Sales Act	20
Chapter 25B - Credit	20
Chapter 25C - Sales of Artwork	20
Chapter 26 - Suretyship	20
Chapter 27 - Warehouse Receipts [Repealed.]	20
Chapter 28 - Administration [Repealed.]	20
Chapter 28A - Administration of Decedents' Estates	20
Chapter 28B - Estates of Absentees in Military Service	20
Chapter 28C - Estates of Missing Persons	20
Chapter 29 - Intestate Succession	21
Chapter 30 - Surviving Spouses	21
Chapter 31 - Wills	21
Chapter 31A - Acts Barring Property Rights	21
Chapter 31B - Renunciation of Property and Renunciation of Fiduciary Powers Act	21
Chapter 31C - Uniform Disposition of Community Property Rights at Death Act	21
Chapter 32 - Fiduciaries	21
Chapter 32A - Powers of Attorney	21
Chapter 33 - Guardian and Ward [Repealed and Recodified.]	21

Chapter 33A - North Carolina Uniform Transfers to Minors Act	21
Chapter 33B - North Carolina Uniform Custodial Trust Act	21
Chapter 34 - Veterans' Guardianship Act	22
Chapter 35 - Sterilization Procedures	22
Chapter 35A - Incompetency and Guardianship	22
Chapter 36 - Trusts and Trustees [Repealed.]	22
Chapter 36A - Trusts and Trustees	22
Chapter 36B - Uniform Management of Institutional Funds Act [Repealed.]	22
Chapter 36C - North Carolina Uniform Trust Code	22
Chapter 36D - North Carolina Community Third Party Trusts, Pooled Trusts	23
Chapter 36E - Uniform Prudent Management of Institutional Funds Act	23
Chapter 37 - Allocation of Principal and Income [Repealed.]	23
Chapter 37A - Uniform Principal and Income Act	23
Chapter 38 - Boundaries	23
Chapter 38A - Landowner Liability	23
Chapter 38B - Trespasser Responsibility	23
Chapter 39 - Conveyances	23
Chapter 39A - Transfer Fee Covenants Prohibited	23
Chapter 40 - Eminent Domain [Repealed.]	23
Chapter 40A - Eminent Domain	23
Chapter 41 - Estates	23
Chapter 41A - State Fair Housing Act	23
Chapter 42 - Landlord and Tenant	23
Chapter 42A - Vacation Rental Act	23
Chapter 43 - Land Registration	23
Chapter 44 - Liens	24
Chapter 44A - Statutory Liens and Charges	24
Chapter 45 - Mortgages and Deeds of Trust	24
Chapter 45A - Good Funds Settlement Act	24
Chapter 46 - Partition	24
Chapter 47 - Probate and Registration	25
Chapter 47A - Unit Ownership	25
Chapter 47B - Real Property Marketable Title Act	25
Chapter 47C - North Carolina Condominium Act	25
Chapter 47D - Notice of Settlement Act [Expired.]	25
Chapter 47E - Residential Property Disclosure Act	25
Chapter 47F - North Carolina Planned Community Act	25
Chapter 47G - Option to Purchase Contracts	25
Chapter 47H - Contracts for Deed	25
Chapter 48 - Adoptions +	26
Chapter 48A - Minors	26
Chapter 49 - Bastardy	26
Chapter 49A - Rights of Children	26
Chapter 50 - Divorce and Alimony	26

Chapter 50A - Uniform Child-Custody Jurisdiction and Enforcement Act	26
Chapter 50B - Domestic Violence	26
Chapter 50C - Civil No-Contact Orders	26
Chapter 51 - Marriage	26
Chapter 52 - Powers and Liabilities of Married Persons	27
Chapter 52A - Uniform Reciprocal Enforcement of Support Act [Repealed.]	27
Chapter 52B - Uniform Premarital Agreement Act	27
Chapter 52C - Uniform Interstate Family Support Act	27
Chapter 53 - Banks	27
Chapter 53A - Business Development Corporations and North Carolina Capital Resource Corporations	28
Chapter 53B - Financial Privacy Act	28
Chapter 54 - Cooperative Organizations	28
Chapter 54A - Capital Stock Savings and Loan Associations [Repealed.]	28
Chapter 54B - Savings and Loan Associations	29
Chapter 54C - Savings Banks	29
Chapter 55 - North Carolina Business Corporation Act	30
Chapter 55A - North Carolina Nonprofit Corporation Act	31
Chapter 55B - Professional Corporation Act	31
Chapter 55C - Foreign Trade Zones	31
Chapter 55D - Filings, Names, and Registered Agents for Corporations, Nonprofit Corporations, and Partnerships	31
Chapter 56 - Electric, Telegraph and Power Companies [Repealed.]	31
Chapter 57 - Hospital, Medical and Dental Service Corporations [Recodified.]	31
Chapter 57A - Health Maintenance Organization Act [Recodified.]	31
Chapter 57B - Health Maintenance Organization Act [Recodified.]	31
Chapter 57C - North Carolina Limited Liability Company Act.	31
Chapter 58 - Insurance.	32
Chapter 58 - Insurance (Continuation)	33
Chapter 58 - Insurance (Continuation)	34
Chapter 58 - Insurance (Continuation)	35
Chapter 58 - Insurance (Continuation)	36
Chapter 58 - Insurance (Continuation)	37
Chapter 58 - Insurance (Continuation)	38
Chapter 58A - North Carolina Health Insurance Trust Commission [Recodified.]	38
Chapter 59 - Partnership.	39
Chapter 59B - Uniform Unincorporated Nonprofit Association Act.	39
Chapter 60 - Railroads and Other Carriers [Repealed and Transferred.]	39
Chapter 61 - Religious Societies	39
Chapter 62 - Public Utilities	39

Chapter 62 - Public Utilities (Continuation)	40
Chapter 62A - Public Safety Telephone Service And Wireless Telephone Service	40
Chapter 63 - Aeronautics	40
Chapter 63A - North Carolina Global TransPark Authority	40
Chapter 64 - Aliens	40
Chapter 65 – Cemeteries	40
Chapter 66 - Commerce and Business	41
Chapter 67 - Dogs	41
Chapter 68 - Fences and Stock Law	41
Chapter 69 - Fire Protection	41
Chapter 70 - Indian Antiquities, Archaeological Resources and Unmarked Human Skeletal Remains Protection	42
Chapter 71 - Indians [Repealed.]	42
Chapter 71A - Indians	42
Chapter 72 - Inns, Hotels and Restaurants	42
Chapter 73 - Mills	42
Chapter 74 - Mines and Quarries	42
Chapter 74A - Company Police [Repealed.]	42
Chapter 74B - Private Protective Services Act [Repealed.]	42
Chapter 74C - Private Protective Services	42
Chapter 74D - Alarm Systems	42
Chapter 74E - Company Police Act	42
Chapter 74F - Locksmith Licensing Act	42
Chapter 74G - Campus Police Act	42
Chapter 75 - Monopolies, Trusts and Consumer Protection	42
Chapter 75A - Boating and Water Safety	43
Chapter 75B - Discrimination in Business	43
Chapter 75C - Motion Picture Fair Competition Act	43
Chapter 75D - Racketeer Influenced and Corrupt Organizations	43
Chapter 75E - Unlawful Activities in Connection With Certain Corporate Transactions	43
Chapter 76 - Navigation	43
Chapter 76A - Navigation and Pilotage Commissions	43
Chapter 77 - Rivers, Creeks, and Coastal Waters	43
Chapter 78 - Securities Law [Repealed.]	43
Chapter 78A - North Carolina Securities Act	43
Chapter 78B - Tender Offer Disclosure Act [Repealed.]	43
Chapter 78C - Investment Advisers	43
Chapter 78D - Commodities Act	43
Chapter 79 - Strays [Repealed.]	43
Chapter 80 - Trademarks, Brands, etc.	44
Chapter 81 - Weights and Measures [Recodified.]	44
Chapter 81A - Weights and Measures Act of 1975.	44
Chapter 82 - Wrecks [Repealed.]	44
Chapter 83 - Architects [Recodified.]	44

Chapter 83A - Architects	44
Chapter 84 - Attorneys-at-Law	44
Chapter 84A - Foreign Legal Consultants	44
Chapter 85 - Auctions and Auctioneers [Repealed.]	44
Chapter 85A - Bail Bondsmen and Runners [Recodified.]	44
Chapter 85B - Auctions and Auctioneers	44
Chapter 85C - Bail Bondsmen and Runners [Recodified.]	44
Chapter 86 - Barbers [Recodified.]	44
Chapter 86A - Barbers	44
Chapter 87 - Contractors	44
Chapter 88 - Cosmetic Art [Repealed.]	44
Chapter 88A - Electrolysis Practice Act	44
Chapter 88B - Cosmetic Art	45
Chapter 89 - Engineering and Land Surveying [Recodified.]	45
Chapter 89A - Landscape Architects	45
Chapter 89B - Foresters	45
Chapter 89C - Engineering and Land Surveying	45
Chapter 89D - Landscape Contractors	45
Chapter 89E - Geologists Licensing Act	45
Chapter 89F - North Carolina Soil Scientist Licensing Act	45
Chapter 89G - Irrigation Contractors	45
Chapter 90 - Medicine and Allied Occupations	45
Chapter 90 - Medicine and Allied Occupations (Continuation)	46
Chapter 90 - Medicine and Allied Occupations (Continuation)	47
Chapter 90 - Medicine and Allied Occupations (Continuation)	48
Chapter 90A - Sanitarians and Water and Wastewater Treatment Facility Operators	48
Chapter 90B - Social Worker Certification and Licensure Act	48
Chapter 90C - North Carolina Recreational Therapy Licensure Act	48
Chapter 90D - Interpreters and Transliterators	48
Chapter 91 - Pawnbrokers [Repealed.]	48
Chapter 91A - Pawnbrokers Modernization Act of 1989	48
Chapter 92 - Photographers [Deleted.]	48
Chapter 93 - Certified Public Accountants	48
Chapter 93A - Real Estate License Law	49
Chapter 93B - Occupational Licensing Boards	49
Chapter 93C - Watchmakers [Repealed.]	49
Chapter 93D - North Carolina State Hearing Aid Dealers and Fitters Board.	49
Chapter 93E - North Carolina Appraisers Act	49
Chapter 94 - Apprenticeship	49
Chapter 95 - Department of Labor and Labor Regulations	49
Chapter 95 - Department of Labor and Labor Regulations (Continuation)	50
Chapter 96 - Employment Security	50
Chapter 97 - Workers' Compensation Act	50
Chapter 97 - Workers' Compensation Act (Continuation)	51

Chapter 98 - Burnt and Lost Records	51
Chapter 99 - Libel and Slander	51
Chapter 99A - Civil Remedies for Criminal Actions	51
Chapter 99B - Products Liability	51
Chapter 99C - Actions Relating to Winter Sports Safety and Accidents	51
Chapter 99D - Civil Rights	51
Chapter 99E - Special Liability Provisions	51
Chapter 100 - Monuments, Memorials and Parks	51
Chapter 101 - Names of Persons	51
Chapter 102 - Official Survey Base	51
Chapter 103 - Sundays, Holidays and Special Days	51
Chapter 104 - United States Lands	51
Chapter 104A - Degrees of Kinship	51
Chapter 104B - Hurricanes or Other Acts of Nature	51
Chapter 104C - Atomic Energy, Radioactivity and Ionizing Radiation [Repealed and Recodified.]	51
Chapter 104D - Southern States Energy Compact	51
Chapter 104E - North Carolina Radiation Protection Act	51
Chapter 104F - Southeast Interstate Low-Level Radioactive Waste Management Compact [Repealed]	51
Chapter 104G - North Carolina Low-Level Radioactive Waste Management Authority Act of 1987 [Repealed]	51
Chapter 105 - Taxation	51
Chapter 105 - Taxation (Continuation)	52
Chapter 105 - Taxation (Continuation)	53
Chapter 105 - Taxation (Continuation)	54
Chapter 105A - Setoff Debt Collection Act	55
Chapter 105B - Defaulted Student Loan Recovery Act	55
Chapter 106 - Agriculture	55
Chapter 106 - Agriculture (Continue)	56
Chapter 106 - Agriculture (Continue)	57
Chapter 107 - Agricultural Development Districts [Repealed.]	57
Chapter 108 - Social Services [Repealed and Recodified.]	57
Chapter 108A - Social Services	57
Chapter 108B - Community Action Programs	58
Chapter 108C Medicaid and Health Choice Provider Requirements.	58
Chapter 108D Medicaid Managed Care for Behavioral Health Services.	58
Chapter 109 - Bonds [Recodified.]	58
Chapter 110 - Child Welfare	58
Chapter 111 - Aid to the Blind	58
Chapter 112 - Confederate Homes and Pensions [Repealed.]	58
Chapter 113 - Conservation and Development	58
Chapter 113 - Conservation and Development (Continuation)	59

Chapter 113A - Pollution Control and Environment	59
Chapter 113A - Pollution Control and Environment (Continuation)	60
Chapter 113B - North Carolina Energy Policy Act of 1975	60
Chapter 114 - Department of Justice	60
Chapter 115 - Elementary and Secondary Education [Repealed.]	60
Chapter 115A - Community Colleges, Technical Institutes, and Industrial Education Centers [Repealed.]	60
Chapter 115B - Tuition and Fee Waivers	60
Chapter 115C - Elementary and Secondary Education	60
Chapter 115C - Elementary and Secondary Education (Continuation)	61
Chapter 115C - Elementary and Secondary Education (Continuation)	62
Chapter 115C - Elementary and Secondary Education (Continuation)	63
Chapter 115D - Community Colleges	63
Chapter 115E - Private Educational Facilities Finance Act [Recodified]	63
Chapter 116 - Higher Education	63
Chapter 116 - Higher Education (Continuation)	63
Chapter 116A - Escheats and Abandoned Property [Repealed.]	64
Chapter 116B - Escheats and Abandoned Property	64
Chapter 116C - Continuum of Education Programs	64
Chapter 116D - Higher Education Bonds	64
Chapter 117 - Electrification	64
Chapter 118 - Firemen's and Rescue Squad Workers' Relief and Pension Funds [Recodified.]	64
Chapter 118A - Firemen's Death Benefit Act [Repealed.]	64
Chapter 118B - Members of a Rescue Squad Death Benefit Act [Repealed.]	64
Chapter 119 - Gasoline and Oil Inspection and Regulation	64
Chapter 120 - General Assembly	65
Chapter 120 - General Assembly (Continuation)	66
Chapter 120 - General Assembly (Continuation)	67
Chapter 120C - Lobbying	67
Chapter 121 - Archives and History	67
Chapter 122 - Hospitals for the Mentally Disordered [Repealed.]	67
Chapter 122A - North Carolina Housing Finance Agency	67
Chapter 122B - North Carolina Agricultural Facilities Finance Act [Repealed.]	67
Chapter 122C - Mental Health, Developmental Disabilities, and Substance Abuse Act of 1985	67
Chapter 122C - Mental Health, Developmental Disabilities, and Substance Abuse Act of 1985 (Continuation)	68
Chapter 122D - North Carolina Agricultural Finance Act	68

Chapter 122E - North Carolina Housing Trust and Oil Overcharge Act	68
Chapter 123 - Impeachment	69
Chapter 123A - Industrial Development [Repealed.]	69
Chapter 124 - Internal Improvements	69
Chapter 125 - Libraries	69
Chapter 126 - State Personnel System	69
Chapter 127 - Militia [Repealed.]	69
Chapter 127A - Militia	69
Chapter 127B - Military Affairs	69
Chapter 127C - Advisory Commission on Military Affairs	69
Chapter 128 - Offices and Public Officers	69
Chapter 128 - Offices and Public Officers (Continuation)	70
Chapter 129 - Public Buildings and Grounds	70
Chapter 130 - Public Health [Repealed.]	70
Chapter 130A - Public Health	70
Chapter 130A - Public Health (Continuation)	71
Chapter 130A - Public Health (Continuation)	72
Chapter 130B - Hazardous Waste Management Commission [Repealed.]	72
Chapter 131 - Public Hospitals [Repealed.]	72
Chapter 131A - Health Care Facilities Finance Act	72
Chapter 131B - Licensing of Ambulatory Surgical Facilities [Repealed.]	72
Chapter 131C - Charitable Solicitation Licensure Act [Repealed.]	72
Chapter 131D - Inspection and Licensing of Facilities	72
Chapter 131E - Health Care Facilities and Services	72
Chapter 131E - Health Care Facilities and Services (Continuation)	73
Chapter 131F - Solicitation of Contributions	73
Chapter 132 - Public Records	73
Chapter 133 - Public Works	74
Chapter 134 - Youth Development [Recodified.]	74
Chapter 134A - Youth Services [Repealed.]	74
Chapter 135 - Retirement System for Teachers and State Employees; Social Security; Health Insurance Program for Children	74
Chapter 135 - Retirement System for Teachers and State Employees; Social Security; Health Insurance Program for Children	75
Chapter 136 - Transportation	75
Chapter 136 - Transportation (Continuation)	76
Chapter 137 - Rural Rehabilitation [Repealed.]	76
Chapter 138 - Salaries, Fees and Allowances	76
Chapter 138A - State Government Ethics Act	76
Chapter 139 - Soil and Water Conservation Districts	76

Chapter 140 - State Art Museum; Symphony and Art Societies	76
Chapter 140A - State Awards System	76
Chapter 141 - State Boundaries	76
Chapter 142 - State Debt	76
Chapter 143 - State Departments, Institutions, and Commissions	77
Chapter 143 - State Departments, Institutions, and Commissions (Continuation)	78
Chapter 143 - State Departments, Institutions, and Commissions (Continuation)	79
Chapter 143 - State Departments, Institutions, and Commissions (Continuation)	80
Chapter 143A - State Government Reorganization	80
Chapter 143B - Executive Organization Act of 1973	80
Chapter 143B - Executive Organization Act of 1973 (Continuation)	81
Chapter 143B - Executive Organization Act of 1973 (Continuation)	82
Chapter 143C - State Budget Act	83
Chapter 143D - The State Governmental Accountability and Internal Control Act	83
Chapter 144 - State Flag, Official Governmental Flags, Motto, and Colors	83
Chapter 145 - State Symbols and Other Official Adoptions.	83
Chapter 146 - State Lands	83
Chapter 147 - State Officers	83
Chapter 148 - State Prison System	84
Chapter 149 - State Song and Toast	84
Chapter 150 - Uniform Revocation of Licenses [Repealed.]	84
Chapter 150A - Administrative Procedure Act [Recodified.]	84
Chapter 150B - Administrative Procedure Act	84
Chapter 151 - Constables [Repealed.]	84
Chapter 152 - Coroners	84
Chapter 152A - County Medical Examiner [Repealed.]	84
Chapter 152A - County Medical Examiner [Repealed.] (Continuation)	85
Chapter 153 - Counties and County Commissioners [Repealed.]	85
Chapter 153A - Counties	85
Chapter 153B - Mountain Resources Planning Act	85
Chapter 153C - Uwharrie Regional Resources Act	85
Chapter 154 - County Surveyor [Repealed.]	85
Chapter 155 - County Treasurer [Repealed.]	85
Chapter 156 - Drainage	85
Chapter 156 – Drainage (Continuation)	86

Chapter 157 - Housing Authorities and Projects	86
Chapter 157A - Historic Properties Commissions [Transferred.]	86
Chapter 158 - Local Development	86
Chapter 159 - Local Government Finance	86
Chapter 159 - Local Government Finance (Continuation)	87
Chapter 159A - Pollution Abatement and Industrial Facilities Financing Act [Unconstitutional.]	87
Chapter 159B - Joint Municipal Electric Power and Energy Act	87
Chapter 159C - Industrial and Pollution Control Facilities Financing Act	87
Chapter 159D - The North Carolina Capital Facilities Financing Act	87
Chapter 159E - Registered Public Obligations Act	87
Chapter 159F - North Carolina Energy Development Authority [Repealed.]	87
Chapter 159G - Water Infrastructure	87
Chapter 159H - [Reserved.]	87
Chapter 159I - Solid Waste Management Loan Program and Local Government Special Obligation Bonds	87
Chapter 160 - Municipal Corporations [Repealed And Transferred.]	87
Chapter 160A - Cities and Towns	88
Chapter 160A - Cities and Towns (Continuation)	89
Chapter 160B - Consolidated City-County Act	89
Chapter 160C - Baseball Park Districts [Repealed.]	90
Chapter 161 - Register of Deeds	90
Chapter 162 - Sheriff	90
Chapter 162A - Water and Sewer Systems	90
Chapter 162B Continuity of Local Government in Emergency.	90
Chapter 163 Elections and Election Laws.	90
Chapter 163 Elections and Election Laws. (Continuation)	91
Chapter 164 Concerning the General Statutes of North Carolina.	92
Chapter 165 Veterans.	92
Chapter 166 Civil Preparedness Agencies [Repealed.]	92
Chapter 166A North Carolina Emergency Management Act.	92
Chapter 167 State Civil Air Patrol [Repealed.]	92
Chapter 168 Persons with Disabilities.	92
Chapter 168A Persons With Disabilities Protection Act.	92

Chapter 29

Intestate Succession.

Article 1.

General Provisions.

§ 29-1. Short title.

This Chapter shall be known and may be cited as the Intestate Succession Act. (1959, c. 879, s. 1.)

§ 29-2. Definitions.

As used in this Chapter, unless the context otherwise requires, the term:

(1) "Advancement" means an irrevocable inter vivos gift of property, made by an intestate donor to any person who would be the donor's heir or one of the donor's heirs upon the donor's death, and intended by the intestate donor to enable the donee to anticipate the donee's inheritance to the extent of the gift; except that no gift to a spouse shall be considered an advancement unless so designated by the intestate donor in a writing signed by the donor at the time of the gift.

(2) "Estate" means all the property of a decedent, including but not limited to:

a. An estate for the life of another; and

b. All future interests in property not terminable by the death of the owner thereof, including all reversions, remainders, executory interests, rights of entry and possibilities of reverter, subject, however, to all limitations and conditions imposed upon such future interests.

(3) "Heir" means any person entitled to take real or personal property upon intestacy under the provisions of this Chapter.

(4) "Lineal descendants" of a person means all children of such person and successive generations of children of such children.

(5) "Net estate" means the estate of a decedent, exclusive of family allowances, costs of administration, and all lawful claims against the estate.

(6) "Share," when used to describe the share of a net estate or property which any person is entitled to take, includes both the fractional share of the personal property and the undivided fractional interest in the real property, which the person is entitled to take. (1959, c. 879, s. 1; 1961, c. 958, s. 1; 2011-344, s. 5.)

§ 29-3. Certain distinctions as to intestate succession abolished.

In the determination of those persons who take upon intestate succession there is no distinction:

(1) Between real and personal property, or

(2) Between ancestral and nonancestral property, or

(3) Between relations of the whole blood and those of the half blood. (1959, c. 879, s. 1.)

§ 29-4. Curtesy and dower abolished.

The estates of curtesy and dower are hereby abolished. (1959, c. 879, s. 1.)

§ 29-5. Computation of next of kin.

Degrees of kinship shall be computed as provided in G.S. 104A-1. (1959, c. 879, s. 1.)

§ 29-6. Lineal succession unlimited.

There shall be no limitation on the right of succession by lineal descendants of an intestate. (1959, c. 879, s. 1.)

§ 29-7. Collateral succession limited.

There shall be no right of succession by collateral kin who are more than five degrees of kinship removed from an intestate; provided that if there is no collateral relative within the five degrees of kinship referred to herein, then collateral succession shall be unlimited to prevent any property from escheating. (1959, c. 879, s. 1.)

§ 29-8. Partial intestacy.

If part but not all of the estate of a decedent is validly disposed of by the decedent's will, the part not disposed of by such will shall descend and be distributed as intestate property. (1959, c. 879, s. 1; 2011-344, s. 5.)

§ 29-9. Inheritance by unborn infant.

Lineal descendants and other relatives of an intestate born within 10 lunar months after the death of the intestate, shall inherit as if they had been born in the lifetime of the intestate and had survived him. (1959, c. 879, s. 1.)

§ 29-10. Renunciation.

Renunciation of an intestate share shall be as provided for in Chapter 31B of the General Statutes. (1959, c. 879, s. 1; 1961, c. 958, s. 2; 1975, c. 371, s. 2.)

§ 29-11. Aliens.

Unless otherwise provided by law, it shall be no bar to intestate succession by any person, that the person, or any other person through whom the person traces the person's inheritance, is or has been an alien. (1959, c. 879, s. 1; 2011-344, s. 5.)

§ 29-12. Escheats.

If there is no person entitled to take under G.S. 29-14 or G.S. 29-15, or if in case of an intestate born out of wedlock, there is no one entitled to take under G.S. 29-21 or G.S. 29-22, the net estate shall escheat as provided in G.S. 116B-2. (1959, c. 879, s. 1; 1961, c. 83; 1973, c. 1446, s. 7; 1999-456, s. 1; 1999-460, s. 8; 2013-198, s. 6.)

§ 29-12.1. Controversies under this Chapter.

Any controversy arising under this Chapter shall be determined as an estate proceeding under Article 2 of Chapter 28A of the General Statutes, except that controversies arising under Article 8 of this Chapter shall be determined as set forth in that Chapter. (2011-344, s. 5.)

Article 2.

Shares of Persons Who Take upon Intestacy.

§ 29-13. Descent and distribution upon intestacy; 120-hour survivorship requirement, revised simultaneous death act, Article 24, Chapter 28A.

(a) All the estate of a person dying intestate shall descend and be distributed, subject to the payment of costs of administration and other lawful claims against the estate, and subject to the payment of State inheritance or estate taxes, as provided in this Chapter.

(b) The determination of whether an heir has predeceased a person dying intestate shall be made as provided by Article 24 of Chapter 28A of the General Statutes. (1959, c. 879, s. 1; 1999-337, s. 5; 2007-132, s. 2.)

§ 29-14. Share of surviving spouse.

(a) Real Property. - The share of the surviving spouse in the real property is:

(1) If the intestate is survived by only one child or by any lineal descendant of only one deceased child, a one-half undivided interest in the real property;

(2) If the intestate is survived by two or more children, or by one child and any lineal descendant of one or more deceased children or by lineal descendants of two or more deceased children, a one-third undivided interest in the real property;

(3) If the intestate is not survived by a child, children or any lineal descendant of a deceased child or children, but is survived by one or more parents, a one-half undivided interest in the real property;

(4) If the intestate is not survived by a child, children or any lineal descendant of a deceased child or children, or by a parent, all the real property.

(b) The share of the surviving spouse in the personal property is:

(1) If the intestate is survived by only one child or by any lineal descendant of only one deceased child, and the net personal property does not exceed sixty thousand dollars ($60,000) in value, all of the personal property; if the net personal property exceeds sixty thousand dollars ($60,000) in value, the sum of sixty thousand dollars ($60,000) plus one half of the balance of the personal property;

(2) If the intestate is survived by two or more children, or by one child and any lineal descendant of one or more deceased children, or by lineal descendants of two or more deceased children, and the net personal property does not exceed sixty thousand dollars ($60,000) in value, all of the personal property; if the net personal property exceeds sixty thousand dollars ($60,000)

in value, the sum of sixty thousand dollars ($60,000) plus one third of the balance of the personal property;

(3)   If the intestate is not survived by a child, children, or any lineal descendant of a deceased child or children, but is survived by one or more parents, and the net personal property does not exceed one hundred thousand dollars ($100,000) in value, all of the personal property; if the net personal property exceeds one hundred thousand dollars ($100,000) in value, the sum of one hundred thousand dollars ($100,000) plus one half of the balance of the personal property;

(4)   If the intestate is not survived by a child, children, or any lineal descendant of a deceased child or children, or by a parent, all of the personal property.

(c)   When an equitable distribution of property is awarded to the surviving spouse pursuant to G.S. 50-20 subsequent to the death of the decedent, the share of the surviving spouse determined under subsections (a) and (b) of this section shall be first determined as though no property had been awarded to the surviving spouse pursuant to G.S. 50-20 subsequent to the death of the decedent, and then reduced by the net value of the marital estate awarded to the surviving spouse pursuant to G.S. 50-20 subsequent to the death of the decedent. (1959, c. 879, s. 1; 1979, c. 186, s. 1; 1981, c. 69; 1995, c. 262, s. 3; 2001-364, s. 6; 2012-71, s. 1.)

§ 29-15. Shares of others than surviving spouse.

Those persons surviving the intestate, other than the surviving spouse, shall take that share of the net estate not distributable to the surviving spouse, or the entire net estate if there is no surviving spouse, as follows:

(1)   If the intestate is survived by only one child or by only one lineal descendant of only one deceased child, that person shall take the entire net estate or share, but if the intestate is survived by two or more lineal descendants of only one deceased child, they shall take as provided in G.S. 29-16; or

(2)   If the intestate is survived by two or more children or by one child and any lineal descendant of one or more deceased children, or by lineal

descendants of two or more deceased children, they shall take as provided in G.S. 29-16; or

(3)   If the intestate is not survived by a child, children or any lineal descendant of a deceased child or children, but is survived by both parents, they shall take in equal shares, or if either parent is dead, the surviving parent shall take the entire share; or

(4)   If the intestate is not survived by such children or lineal descendants or by a parent, the brothers and sisters of the intestate, and the lineal descendants of any deceased brothers or sisters, shall take as provided in G.S. 29-16; or

(5)   If there is no one entitled to take under the preceding subdivisions of this section or under G.S. 29-14,

a.   The paternal grandparents shall take one half of the net estate in equal shares, or, if either is dead, the survivor shall take the entire one half of the net estate, and if neither paternal grandparent survives, then the paternal uncles and aunts of the intestate and the lineal descendants of deceased paternal uncles and aunts shall take said one half as provided in G.S. 29-16; and

b.   The maternal grandparents shall take the other one half in equal shares, or if either is dead, the survivor shall take the entire one half of the net estate, and if neither maternal grandparent survives, then the maternal uncles and aunts of the intestate and the lineal descendants of deceased maternal uncles and aunts shall take one half as provided in G.S. 29-16; but

c.   If there is no grandparent and no uncle or aunt, or lineal descendant of a deceased uncle or aunt, on the paternal side, then those of the maternal side who otherwise would be entitled to take one half as hereinbefore provided in this subdivision shall take the whole; or

d.   If there is no grandparent and no uncle or aunt, or lineal descendant of a deceased uncle or aunt, on the maternal side, then those on the paternal side who otherwise would be entitled to take one half as hereinbefore provided in this subdivision shall take the whole. (1959, c. 879, s. 1.)

Article 3.

Distribution among Classes.

§ 29-16. Distribution among classes.

(a) Children and Their Lineal Descendants. - If the intestate is survived by lineal descendants, their respective shares in the property which they are entitled to take under G.S. 29-15 of this Chapter shall be determined in the following manner:

(1) Children. - To determine the share of each surviving child, divide the property by the number of surviving children plus the number of deceased children who have left lineal descendants surviving the intestate.

(2) Grandchildren. - To determine the share of each surviving grandchild by a deceased child of the intestate in the property not taken under the preceding subdivision of this subsection, divide that property by the number of such surviving grandchildren plus the number of deceased grandchildren who have left lineal descendants surviving the intestate.

(3) Great-Grandchildren. - To determine the share of each surviving great-grandchild by a deceased grandchild of the intestate in the property not taken under the preceding subdivisions of this subsection, divide that property by the number of such surviving great-grandchildren plus the number of deceased great-grandchildren who have left lineal descendants surviving the intestate.

(4) Great-Great-Grandchildren. - To determine the share of each surviving great-great-grandchild by a deceased great-grandchild of the intestate in the property not taken under the preceding subdivisions of this subsection, divide that property by the number of such surviving great-great-grandchildren plus the number of deceased great-great-grandchildren who have left lineal descendants surviving the intestate.

(5) Other Lineal Descendants of Children. - Divide, according to the formula established in the preceding subdivisions of this subsection, any property not taken under such preceding subdivisions, among the lineal descendants of the children of the intestate not already participating.

(b) Brothers and Sisters and Their Lineal Descendants. - If the intestate is survived by brothers and sisters or the lineal descendants of deceased brothers and sisters, their respective shares in the property which they are entitled to take under G.S. 29-15 of this Chapter shall be determined in the following manner:

(1) Brothers and Sisters. - To determine the share of each surviving brother and sister, divide the property by the number of surviving brothers and sisters plus the number of deceased brothers and sisters who have left lineal descendants surviving the intestate within the fifth degree of kinship to the intestate.

(2) Nephews and Nieces. - To determine the share of each surviving nephew or niece by a deceased brother or sister of the intestate in the property not taken under the preceding subdivision of this subsection, divide that property by the number of such surviving nephews or nieces plus the number of deceased nephews and nieces who have left lineal descendants surviving the intestate within the fifth degree of kinship to the intestate.

(3) Grandnephews and Grandnieces. - To determine the share of each surviving grandnephew or grandniece by a deceased nephew or niece of the intestate in the property not taken under the preceding subdivisions of this subsection, divide that property by the number of such surviving grandnephews and grandnieces plus the number of deceased grandnephews and grandnieces who have left children surviving the intestate.

(4) Great-Grandnephews and Great-Grandnieces. - To determine the share of each surviving child of a deceased grandnephew or grandniece of the intestate, divide equally among the great-grandnephews and great-grandnieces of the intestate any property not taken under the preceding subdivisions of this subsection.

(5) Grandparents and Others. - If there is no one within the fifth degree of kinship to the intestate entitled to take the property under the preceding subdivisions of this subsection, then the intestate's property shall go to those entitled to take under G.S. 29-15(5).

(c) Uncles and Aunts and Their Lineal Descendants. - If the intestate is survived by uncles and aunts or the lineal descendants of deceased uncles and aunts, their respective shares in the property which they are entitled to take under G.S. 29-15 shall be determined in the following manner:

(1) Uncles and Aunts. - To determine the share of each surviving uncle and aunt, divide the property by the number of surviving uncles and aunts plus the number of deceased uncles and aunts who have left children or grandchildren surviving the intestate.

(2) Children of Uncles and Aunts. - To determine the share of each surviving child of a deceased uncle or aunt of the intestate in the property not taken under the preceding subdivision of this subsection, divide that property by the number of surviving children of deceased uncles and aunts plus the number of deceased children of deceased uncles and aunts who have left children surviving the intestate.

(3) Grandchildren of Uncles and Aunts. - To determine the share of each surviving child of a deceased child of a deceased uncle or aunt of the intestate, divide equally among the grandchildren of uncles or aunts of the intestate any property not taken under the preceding subdivisions of this subsection. (1959, c. 879, s. 1; 1979, c. 107, ss. 2, 3.)

Article 4.

Adopted Children.

§ 29-17. Succession by, through and from adopted children.

(a) A child, adopted in accordance with Chapter 48 of the General Statutes or in accordance with the applicable law of any other jurisdiction, and the heirs of such child, are entitled by succession to any property by, through and from the child's adoptive parents and their heirs the same as if the child were the natural legitimate child of the adoptive parents.

(b) An adopted child is not entitled by succession to any property, by, through, or from the child's natural parents or their heirs, except as provided in subsection (e) of this section.

(c) The adoptive parents and the heirs of the adoptive parents are entitled by succession to any property, by, through and from an adopted child the same as if the adopted child were the natural legitimate child of the adoptive parents.

(d) The natural parents and the heirs of the natural parents are not entitled by succession to any property, by, through or from an adopted child, except as provided in subsection (e) of this section.

(e) If a natural parent has previously married, is married to, or shall marry an adoptive parent, the adopted child is considered the child of such natural parent for all purposes of intestate succession. (1959, c. 879, s. 1; 2011-344, s. 5.)

Article 5.

Legitimated Children.

§ 29-18. Succession by, through and from legitimated children.

A child born out of wedlock who has been legitimated in accordance with G.S. 49-10 or 49-12 or in accordance with the applicable law of any other jurisdiction, and the heirs of the child, are entitled by succession to property by, through and from the child's father and mother and their heirs the same as if born in lawful wedlock; and if the child dies intestate, the child's property shall descend and be distributed as if the child had been born in lawful wedlock. (1959, c. 879, s. 1; 2011-344, s. 5; 2013-198, s. 7.)

Article 6.

Children Born Out of Wedlock.

§ 29-19. Succession by, through and from children born out of wedlock.

(a) For purposes of intestate succession, a child born out of wedlock shall be treated as if that child were the legitimate child of the child's mother, so that the child and the child's lineal descendants are entitled to take by, through and from the child's mother and the child's other maternal kindred, both descendants and collaterals, and they are entitled to take from the child.

(b) For purposes of intestate succession, a child born out of wedlock shall be entitled to take by, through and from:

(1) Any person who has been finally adjudged to be the father of the child pursuant to the provisions of G.S. 49-1 through 49-9 or the provisions of G.S. 49-14 through 49-16;

(2) Any person who has acknowledged himself during his own lifetime and the child's lifetime to be the father of the child in a written instrument executed or acknowledged before a certifying officer named in G.S. 52-10(b) and filed during his own lifetime and the child's lifetime in the office of the clerk of superior court of the county where either he or the child resides.

(3) A person who died prior to or within one year after the birth of the child and who can be established to have been the father of the child by DNA testing.

Notwithstanding the above provisions, no person shall be entitled to take hereunder unless the person has given written notice of the basis of the person's claim to the personal representative of the putative father within six months after the date of the first publication or posting of the general notice to creditors.

(c) Any person described under subdivision (b)(1), (2), or (3) of this section and the person's lineal and collateral kin shall be entitled to inherit by, through and from the child.

(d) Any person who acknowledges that he is the father of a child born out of wedlock in his duly probated last will shall be deemed to have intended that the child be treated as expressly provided for in the will or, in the absence of any express provision, the same as a legitimate child. (1959, c. 879, s. 1; 1973, c. 1062, s. 1; 1975, c. 54, s. 1; 1977, c. 375, s. 6; c. 591; c. 757, s. 3; 2011-344, s. 5; 2013-198, s. 9.)

§ 29-20. Descent and distribution upon intestacy of children born out of wedlock.

All the estate of a person who was born out of wedlock and dies intestate shall descend and be distributed, subject to the payment of costs of administration and other lawful claims against the estate, and subject to the payment of State inheritance or estate taxes, as provided in this Article. (1959, c. 879, s. 1; 1999-337, s. 6; 2013-198, s. 10.)

§ 29-21. Share of surviving spouse.

The share of the surviving spouse of an intestate born out of wedlock shall be the same as provided in G.S. 29-14 for the surviving spouse of a legitimate person. In determining whether the intestate is survived by one or more parents as provided in G.S. 29-14(3), any person identified as the father under G.S. 29-19(b)(1) or (b)(2) shall be regarded as a parent. (1959, c. 879, s. 1; 1977, c. 757, s. 1; 2013-198, s. 11.)

§ 29-22. Shares of others than the surviving spouse.

Those persons surviving an intestate born out of wedlock, other than the surviving spouse, shall take that share of the net estate provided in G.S. 29-15. In determining whether the intestate is survived by one or more parents or their collateral kindred as provided in G.S. 29-15, any person identified as the father under G.S. 29-19(b)(1) or (b)(2) shall be regarded as a parent. (1959, c. 879, s. 1; 1977, c. 757, s. 2; 2013-198, s. 12.)

Article 7.

Advancements.

§ 29-23. In general.

If a person dies intestate as to all the person's estate, property which the person gave in his lifetime as an advancement shall be counted toward the advancee's intestate share, and to the extent that it does not exceed such intestate share, shall be taken into account in computing the estate to be distributed. (1959, c. 879, s. 1; 2011-344, s. 5.)

§ 29-24. Presumption of gift.

A gratuitous inter vivos transfer is presumed to be an absolute gift and not an advancement unless shown to be an advancement. (1959, c. 879, s. 1.)

§ 29-25. Effect of advancement.

If the amount of the advancement equals or exceeds the intestate share of the advancee, the advancee shall be excluded from any further portion in the distribution of the estate, but the advancee shall not be required to refund any part of such advancement; and if the amount of the advancement is less than the advancee's share, the advancee shall be entitled to such additional amount as will give the advancee the advancee's full share of the intestate donor's estate. (1959, c. 879, s. 1; 2011-344, s. 5.)

§ 29-26. Valuation.

The value of the property given as an advancement shall be determined as of the time when the advancee came into possession or enjoyment, or at the time of the death of the intestate, whichever first occurs. However, if the value of the property, so advanced, is stated by the intestate donor in a writing signed by the intestate donor and designating the gift as an advancement, such value shall be deemed the value of the advancement. (1959, c. 879, s. 1; 2011-344, s. 5.)

§ 29-27. Death of advancee before intestate donor.

If the advancee dies before the intestate donor leaving a lineal heir or heirs who take by intestate succession from the intestate donor, the advancement shall be taken into account in the same manner as if it had been made directly to such heir or heirs, but the value shall be determined as of the time the original advancee came into possession or enjoyment, or when the heir or heirs came into possession or enjoyment or at the time of the death of the intestate donor, whichever first occurs. (1959, c. 879, s. 1; 1961, c. 958, s. 3.)

§ 29-28. Inventory.

If any person who has, in the lifetime of an intestate donor, received a part of the donor's property, refuses, upon order of the clerk of superior court of the county in which the administrator or collector qualifies, to give an inventory on oath, setting forth therein to the best of the person's knowledge and belief the particulars of the transfer of such property, the person shall be considered to have received the person's full share of the donor's estate, and shall not be entitled to receive any further part or share. (1959, c. 879, s. 1; 2011-344, s. 5.)

§ 29-29. Release by advancee.

If the advancee acknowledges to the intestate donor by a signed writing that the advancee has been advanced the advancee's full share of the intestate donor's estate, both the advancee and those claiming through the advancee shall be excluded from any further participation in the intestate donor's estate. (1959, c. 879, s. 1; 2011-344, s. 5.)

Article 8.

Election to Take Life Interest in Lieu of Intestate Share.

§ 29-30. Election of surviving spouse to take life interest in lieu of intestate share provided.

(a) In lieu of the intestate share provided in G.S. 29-14 or G.S. 29-21, or of the elective share provided in G.S. 30-3.1, the surviving spouse of an intestate or the surviving spouse who has petitioned for an elective share shall be entitled to take as the surviving spouse's intestate share or elective share a life estate in one third in value of all the real estate of which the deceased spouse was seised and possessed of an estate of inheritance at any time during coverture, except that real estate as to which the surviving spouse:

(1) Has waived the surviving spouse's rights by joining with the other spouse in a conveyance thereof, or

(2) Has released or quitclaimed the surviving spouse's interest therein in accordance with G.S. 52-10, or

(3) Was not required by law to join in conveyance thereof in order to bar the elective life estate, or

(4) Is otherwise not legally entitled to the election provided in this section.

(b) The surviving spouse may elect to take a life estate in the usual dwelling house occupied by the surviving spouse at the time of the death of the deceased spouse if such dwelling house were owned by the deceased spouse at the time of the deceased spouse's death, together with the outbuildings, improvements and easements thereunto belonging or appertaining, and lands upon which situated and reasonably necessary to the use and enjoyment thereof, as well as a fee simple ownership in the household furnishings therein, despite the fact that a life estate therein might exceed the fractional limitation provided for in subsection (a) of this section. If the value of a life estate in the dwelling house is less than the value of a life estate in one-third in value of all the real estate, the surviving spouse may elect to take a life estate in the dwelling and a life estate in such other real estate as to make the aggregate life estate of the surviving spouse equal to a life estate in one-third in value of all the real estate.

(c) The election provided for in subsection (a) shall be made by the filing of a petition in accordance with Article 2 of Chapter 28A of the General Statutes with the clerk of the superior court of the county in which the administration of the estate is pending, or, if no administration is pending, then with the clerk of the superior court of any county in which the administration of the estate could be commenced. The election shall be made prior to the shorter of the following applicable periods:

(1) In case of testacy, (i) within 12 months of the date of death of the deceased spouse if letters testamentary are not issued within that period, or (ii) within one month after the expiration of the time limit for filing a claim for elective share if letters have been issued.

(2) In case of intestacy, (i) within 12 months after the date of death of the deceased spouse if letters of administration are not issued within that period, or

(ii) within one month after the expiration of the time limit for filing claims against the estate, if letters have been issued.

(3)   Repealed by Session Laws 2011-344, s. 5, effective January 1, 2012.

(4)   If litigation that affects the share of the surviving spouse in the estate is pending, including a pending petition for determination of an elective share, then within such reasonable time as may be allowed by written order of the clerk of the superior court.

(5)   Nothing in this subsection shall extend the period of time for a surviving spouse to petition for an elective share under Article 1A of Chapter 30 of the General Statutes.

(c1)   The petition shall:

(1)   Be directed to the clerk with whom filed;

(2)   State that the surviving spouse making the same elects to take under this section rather than under the provisions of G.S. 29-14, 29-21, or 30-3.1, as applicable;

(3)   Set forth the names of all heirs, devisees, personal representatives and all other persons in possession of or claiming an estate or an interest in the property described in subsection (a); and

(4)   Request the allotment of the life estate provided for in subsection (a).

(c2)   The petition may be filed in person, or by attorney authorized in a writing executed and duly acknowledged by the surviving spouse and attested by at least one witness. If the surviving spouse is a minor or an incompetent, the petition may be executed and filed by a general guardian or by the guardian of the person or estate of the minor or incompetent spouse. If the minor or incompetent spouse has no guardian, the petition may be executed and filed by a guardian ad litem appointed by the clerk. The petition, whether in person or by attorney, shall be filed as a record of the court, and a summons together with a copy of the petition shall be served upon each of the interested persons named in the petition, in accordance with G.S. 1A-1, Rule 4.

(d)   In case of election to take a life estate in lieu of an intestate share or elective share, as provided in either G.S. 29-14, 29-21, or 30-3.3(a), the clerk of superior court, with whom the petition has been filed, shall summon and appoint a jury of three disinterested persons who being first duly sworn shall promptly allot and set apart to the surviving spouse the life estate provided for in subsection (a) and make a final report of such action to the clerk.

(e) The final report shall be filed by the jury not more than 60 days after the summoning and appointment thereof, shall be signed by all jurors, and shall describe by metes and bounds the real estate in which the surviving spouse shall have been allotted and set aside a life estate. It shall be filed as a record of court and a certified copy thereof shall be filed and recorded in the office of the register of deeds of each county in which any part of the real property of the deceased spouse, affected by the allotment, is located.

(f) In the election and procedure to have the life estate allotted and set apart provided for in this section, the rules of procedure relating to partition proceedings under Chapter 46 of the General Statutes shall apply except insofar as the same would be inconsistent with the provisions of this section. A determination of the life estate under this section may be appealed in accordance with G.S. 1-301.3.

(g) Neither the household furnishings in the dwelling house nor the life estates taken by election under this section shall be subject to the payment of debts due from the estate of the deceased spouse, except those debts secured by such property as follows:

(1) By a mortgage or deed of trust in which the surviving spouse has waived the surviving spouse's rights by joining with the other spouse in the making thereof; or

(2) By a purchase money mortgage or deed of trust, or by a conditional sales contract of personal property in which title is retained by the vendor, made prior to or during the marriage; or

(3) By a mortgage or deed of trust made prior to the marriage; or

(4) By a mortgage or deed of trust constituting a lien on the property at the time of its acquisition by the deceased spouse either before or during the marriage.

(h) If no election is made in the manner and within the time provided for in subsection (c) the surviving spouse shall be conclusively deemed to have waived the surviving spouse's right to elect to take under the provisions of this section, and any interest which the surviving spouse may have had in the real estate of the deceased spouse by virtue of this section shall terminate. (1959, c. 879, s. 1; 1961, c. 958, ss. 4-8; 1965, c. 848; 1997-456, s. 27; 2000-178, s. 3; 2011-284, s. 22; 2011-344, s. 5.)

Chapter 30.

Surviving Spouses.

ARTICLE 1.

Dissent from Will.

§§ 30-1 through 30-3: Repealed by Session Laws 2000-178, s. 1.

Article 1A.

Elective Share.

§ 30-3.1. Right of elective share.

(a)   Elective Share. - The surviving spouse of a decedent who dies domiciled in this State has a right to claim an "elective share", which means an amount equal to (i) the applicable share of the Total Net Assets, as defined in G.S. 30-3.2(4), less (ii) the value of Net Property Passing to Surviving Spouse, as defined in G.S. 30-3.2(2c). The applicable share of the Total Net Assets is as follows:

(1)   If the surviving spouse was married to the decedent for less than five years, fifteen percent (15%) of the Total Net Assets.

(2)   If the surviving spouse was married to the decedent for at least five years but less than 10 years, twenty-five percent (25%) of the Total Net Assets.

(3)   If the surviving spouse was married to the decedent for at least 10 years but less than 15 years, thirty-three percent (33%) of the Total Net Assets.

(4) If the surviving spouse was married to the decedent for 15 years or more, fifty percent (50%) of the Total Net Assets.

(b) Repealed by Session Laws 2013-91, s. 1(d), effective October 1, 2013, and applicable to estates of decedents dying on or after October 1, 2013.

(c) Repealed by Session Laws 2009-368, s. 1, effective August 27, 2009, and applicable to decedents dying on or after October 1, 2009. (2000-178, s. 2; 2003-296, s. 1; 2009-368, s. 1; 2013-91, s. 1(d).)

§ 30-3.2. Definitions.

The following definitions apply in this Article:

(1) Claims. - Includes liabilities of the decedent, whether arising in contract, in tort, or otherwise, and liabilities of the decedent's estate that arise at or after the death of the decedent, including funeral and administrative expenses, except for:

a. A claim for equitable distribution of property pursuant to G.S. 50-20 awarded subsequent to the death of the decedent.

b. Death taxes, except for those death taxes attributable to Property Passing to the Surviving Spouse. "Death taxes attributable to Property Passing to the Surviving Spouse" equals the amount of decedent's death taxes as finally determined, less the amount such death taxes would have been if all Property Passing to the Surviving Spouse had qualified for the federal estate tax marital deduction pursuant to section 2056 of the Code or had qualified for a similar provision under the laws of another applicable taxing jurisdiction.

c. A claim founded on a promise or agreement of the decedent, to the extent such claim is not arm's length or is not supported by full or adequate consideration in money or money's worth.

d. Expenses apportioned by the clerk of court under G.S. 30-3.4(h).

(1a) Code. - The Internal Revenue Code in effect at the time of the decedent's death.

(2) Death taxes. - Any estate, inheritance, succession, and similar taxes imposed by any taxing authority, reduced by any applicable credits against those taxes.

(2a) General power of appointment. - Any power of appointment, including a power to designate the beneficiary of a beneficiary designation, exercisable by the decedent, regardless of the decedent's capacity to exercise such power, in favor of the decedent, the decedent's estate, the decedent's creditors, or the creditors of the decedent's estate, except for (i) powers limited by an "ascertainable standard" as defined in G.S. 36C-1-103 and (ii) powers which are not exercisable by the decedent except in conjunction with a person who created the power or has a substantial interest in the property subject to the power and whose interest is adverse to the exercise of the power in favor of the decedent, the decedent's estate, the decedent's creditors, or the creditors of the decedent's estate. In no event shall a power held by the decedent as attorney-in-fact under a power of attorney be considered a general power of appointment.

(2b) Lineal descendant. - Defined in G.S. 29-2.

(2c) Net Property Passing to Surviving Spouse. - The Property Passing to Surviving Spouse reduced by (i) death taxes attributable to property passing to surviving spouse, and (ii) claims payable out of, charged against or otherwise properly allocated to Property Passing to Surviving Spouse.

(3) Nonadverse trustee. - Any of the following:

a. Any person who does not possess a substantial beneficial interest in the trust that would be adversely affected by the exercise or nonexercise of the power that the individual trustee possesses respecting the trust;

b. Any person subject to a power of removal by the surviving spouse with or without cause; or

c. Any company authorized to engage in trust business under the laws of this State, or that otherwise meets the requirements to engage in trust business under the laws of this State.

(3a) Nonspousal assets. - All property included in total assets other than the property included in Property Passing to Surviving Spouse.

(3b) Presently exercisable general power of appointment. - A general power of appointment which is exercisable at the time in question. A testamentary general power of appointment is not presently exercisable.

(3c) Property Passing to Surviving Spouse. - The sum of the values, as valued pursuant to G.S. 30-3.3A, of the following:

a. Property (i) devised, outright or in trust, by the decedent to the surviving spouse or (ii) that passes, outright or in trust, to the surviving spouse by intestacy, beneficiary designation, the exercise or failure to exercise the decedent's testamentary general power of appointment or the decedent's testamentary limited power of appointment, operation of law, or otherwise by reason of the decedent's death, excluding any benefits under the federal social security system.

b. Any year's allowance awarded to the surviving spouse.

c. Property renounced by the surviving spouse.

d. The surviving spouse's interest in any life insurance proceeds on the life of the decedent.

e. Any interest in property, outright or in trust, transferred from the decedent to the surviving spouse during the lifetime of the decedent for which the surviving spouse signs a statement acknowledging such a gift. For purposes of this sub-subdivision, any gift to the surviving spouse by the decedent of the decedent's interest in any property held by the decedent and the surviving spouse as tenants by the entirety or as joint tenants with right of survivorship shall be deemed to be a gift of one-half of the entire interest in property so held by the decedent and the surviving spouse.

f. Property awarded to the surviving spouse, subsequent to the death of the decedent, pursuant to an equitable distribution claim under G.S. 50-20.

g. Property held in a spousal trust described in G.S. 30-3.3A(e)(1).

If property falls under more than one sub-subdivision of this subdivision, then the property shall be included only once, but under the sub-subdivision yielding the greatest value of the property.

(3d) Responsible person. - A person or entity other than the surviving spouse that received, held, or controlled property constituting nonspousal assets on the date used to determine the value of the property. The personal representative is the responsible person for nonspousal assets that pass under the decedent's will or by intestate succession.

(3e) Responsible person's nonspousal assets. - The nonspousal assets received, held, or controlled by a responsible person.

(3f) Total assets. - The sum of the values, as determined pursuant to G.S. 30-3.3A, of the following:

a. The decedent's property that would pass by intestate succession if the decedent died without a will, other than wrongful death proceeds;

b. Property over which the decedent, immediately before death, held a presently exercisable general power of appointment, except for (i) property held jointly with right of survivorship, which is includable in total assets only to the extent provided in sub-subdivision c. of this subdivision and (ii) life insurance, which is includable in Total Assets only to the extent provided in sub-subdivision d. of this subdivision. Includes, without limitation:

1. Property held in a trust that the decedent could revoke.

2. Property held in a trust to the extent that the decedent had an unrestricted power to withdraw the property.

3. Property held in a depository account owned by the decedent in a financial institution payable or transferable at decedent's death to a beneficiary designated by the decedent.

4. Securities owned by the decedent in an account or in certificated form that are payable or transferable at decedent's death to a beneficiary designated by the decedent.

c. Property held as tenants by the entirety or jointly with right of survivorship as follows:

1. One-half of any property held by the decedent and the surviving spouse as tenants by the entirety or as joint tenants with right of survivorship is included, without regard to who contributed the property.

2. Property held by the decedent and one or more other persons other than the surviving spouse as joint tenants with right of survivorship is included to the following extent:

I. All property attributable to the decedent's contribution.

II. The decedent's pro rata share of property not attributable to the decedent's contribution, except to the extent of property attributable to contributions by a surviving joint tenant.

The decedent is presumed to have contributed the jointly owned property unless contribution by another is proven by clear and convincing evidence.

d. Benefits payable by reason of the decedent's death under any policy, plan, contract, or other arrangement, either owned by the decedent or over which the decedent had a general power of appointment or had the power to designate the surviving spouse as beneficiary, including, without limitation:

1. Insurance on the life of the decedent.

2. Accidental death benefits.

3. Annuities.

4. Employee benefits or similar arrangements.

5. Individual retirement accounts.

6. Pension or profit sharing plans.

7. Deferred compensation.

8. Any private or governmental retirement plan.

e. Property irrevocably transferred by the decedent to the extent the decedent retained the possession or enjoyment of, or the right to income from, the property for life or for any period not ascertainable without reference to the decedent's death or for any period that does not in fact end before the decedent's death, except:

1. Property transferred for full and adequate consideration.

2. Transfers to that the surviving spouse consented in writing by signing a deed, an income or gift tax return that reports the gift, or other writing.

3. Transfers that became irrevocable before the decedent's marriage to the surviving spouse.

The property included in total assets is that fraction of the transferred property to which the decedent retained the right.

f. Property transferred by the decedent to the extent the decedent created a power over the property or the income from the property, which, immediately prior to death, could be exercised by the decedent in conjunction with any other person, or which could be exercised by a person who does not have a substantial interest that would be adversely affected by the exercise or nonexercise of the power, for the benefit of the decedent, the decedent's estate, the decedent's creditors, or the creditors of the decedent's estate, except:

1. Property transferred for full and adequate consideration.

2. Transfers to which the surviving spouse consented in writing by signing a deed, an income or gift tax return that reports the gift, or other writing.

3. Transfers which became irrevocable before the decedent's marriage to the surviving spouse.

The property included in total assets with respect to a power over property is that fraction of the property to which the power related.

g. Property transferred by the decedent to persons other than the surviving spouse if such transfer was made both during the one-year period immediately preceding the decedent's death and during the decedent's marriage to the surviving spouse, except:

1. Property transferred for full and adequate consideration.

2. Transfers to which the surviving spouse consented in writing by signing a deed, an income or gift tax return that reports such gift, or other writing.

3. That part of any property transferred to any one transferee that qualified for exclusion from gift tax under section 2503 of the Code.

For purposes of this sub-subdivision, the termination of a right or interest in, or power over, property that would have been included in the total assets under sub-subdivisions b., e., or f. of this subdivision if the right, interest, or power had not terminated until the decedent's death shall be deemed to be a transfer of such property. Termination occurs when, with respect to a right or interest in property, the decedent transfers or relinquishes the right or interest; with respect to a power over property, the power terminates by exercise or release, but not by lapse or default.

If property falls under more than one sub-subdivision of this subdivision, then the property shall be included only once, but under the sub-subdivision yielding the greatest value of the property.

(4) Total Net Assets. - The total assets reduced by year's allowances to persons other than the surviving spouse and claims. (2000-140, s. 92; 2000-178, s. 2; 2001-364, s. 4; 2001-487, s. 16; 2003-296, s. 2; 2009-368, s. 1.)

§ 30-3.3: Repealed by Session Laws 2009-368, s. 1, effective July 27, 2009, and applicable to decedents dying on or after October 1, 2009.

§ 30-3.3A. Valuation of property.

(a) Basic Principles. - Unless otherwise expressly stated to the contrary in this section, the value of property shall be that property's fair market value, taking into consideration any applicable discounts. The value shall be determined as of the date of death, except for (i) property transferred to persons other than the surviving spouse described in G.S. 30-3.2(3f)g. and (ii) property transferred to the surviving spouse described in G.S. 30-3.2(3c)e. that is not held in trust, that is not life insurance, and that is not held as tenants by the entirety or some other form of ownership that passes to the surviving spouse by reason of survivorship. The value of gift property described in clauses (i) and (ii) shall be determined as the value on the date of transfer; but if the donee proves to the satisfaction of the clerk that the value on the date of disposal of the asset prior to the decedent's death is less than on the original date of transfer or that the value on the date of death is less than on the original date of transfer, then the lesser value shall be used.

(b) Certain Joint Property. - In valuing a partial interest in jointly owned property with right of survivorship, there shall be no discount taken to reflect the decedent's partial interest including, but not limited to, discounts for lack of control, ownership of a fractional interest, or lack of marketability.

(c) Certain Powers of Appointment. - In valuing property over which the decedent held a presently exercisable general power of appointment, the value includes only the property subject to the power that passes at the decedent's death, whether by exercise, release, lapse, default, or otherwise.

(d) Certain Transfers With Retained Interests. - In valuing property transferred by the decedent with a retained right of possession or enjoyment or the right to income described in G.S. 30-3.2(3f)e., only the fraction of the property to which the decedent retained a right shall be included. In valuing property in which the decedent created a power as described in G.S. 30-3.2(3f)f., the value includes, with respect to a power, the value of the property subject to the power, and the amount included in the valuation with respect to a power over the income is the value of the property that produces or produced the income; provided, however, if the power is a power over both income and property and the foregoing produces different amounts, the amount included in the valuation is the greater amount.

(e) Partial or Contingent Interest Property. - The valuation of partial and contingent property interests, outright or in trust, which are limited to commence or terminate upon the death of one or more persons, upon the expiration of a period of time, or upon the occurrence of one or more contingencies, shall be determined by computations based upon the mortality and annuity tables set forth in G.S. 8-46 and G.S. 8-47, and by using a presumed rate of return of six percent (6%) of the value of the underlying property in which those interests are limited. However, in valuing partial and contingent interests passing to the surviving spouse, the following special rules apply:

(1) The value of the beneficial interest of a spouse shall be the entire fair market value of any property held in trust if the decedent was the settlor of the trust, if the trust is held for the exclusive benefit of the surviving spouse during the surviving spouse's lifetime, and if the terms of the trust meet the following requirements:

a. During the lifetime of the surviving spouse, the trust is controlled by one or more nonadverse trustees.

b. The trustee shall distribute to or for the benefit of the surviving spouse either (i) the entire net income of the trust at least annually or (ii) the income of the trust in such amounts and at such times as the trustee, in its discretion, determines necessary for the health, maintenance, and support of the surviving spouse.

c. The trustee shall distribute to or for the benefit of the surviving spouse out of the principal of the trust such amounts and at such times as the trustee, in its discretion, determines necessary for the health, maintenance, and support of the surviving spouse.

d. In exercising discretion, the trustee may be authorized or required to take into consideration all other income assets and other means of support available to the surviving spouse.

(2) To the extent that the partial or contingent interest is dependent upon the occurrence of any contingency that is not subject to the control of the surviving spouse and that is not subject to valuation by reference to the mortality and annuity tables set forth in G.S. 8-46 and G.S. 8-47, the contingency will be conclusively presumed to result in the lowest possible value passing to the surviving spouse. However, a life estate or income interest that will terminate upon the surviving spouse's death or remarriage will be valued without regard to the possibility of termination upon remarriage.

(3) To the extent that the valuation of a partial or contingent interest is dependent upon the life expectancy of the surviving spouse, that life expectancy shall be conclusively presumed to be no less than 10 years, regardless of the actual attained age of the surviving spouse at the decedent's death.

(f) Method for Determining Value. - Unless otherwise stated in this Article, the value of property shall be determined as follows:

(1) The value of property passing by intestacy described in G.S. 30-3.2(3f)a. and Property Passing to Surviving Spouse, other than property held in a trust, shall be established by the good-faith agreement of the surviving spouse and the personal representative, unless either (i) the surviving spouse is the personal representative or (ii) the clerk determines that the personal representative may not be able to represent the estate adversely to the

surviving spouse, in which cases the value of such property shall be determined pursuant to subdivision (4) of this subsection.

(2) The value of property constituting an interest in a trust shall be established by good-faith agreement of the surviving spouse, the personal representative, and the trustee, unless either (i) the surviving spouse is both the personal representative and the trustee or (ii) the clerk determines that the trustee or the personal representative may not be able to represent the trust or the estate, respectively, adversely to the surviving spouse, in which cases the value of such property shall be determined pursuant to subdivision (4) of this subsection.

(3) The value of all other property shall be established by the good-faith agreement of the surviving spouse, the personal representative, and the responsible person that received, held, or controlled such property on the date used to determine the value of such property for purposes of determining total assets, unless the clerk determines that valuation under subdivision (4) of this subsection is more appropriate.

(4) If the value of any property is not established by agreement as provided above, the parties may present evidence regarding value, which may include expert testimony, and the clerk may appoint one or more qualified and disinterested persons to help determine the value of such property. After hearing, the clerk shall make a finding of fact of the value of each asset. (2009-368, s. 1.)

§ 30-3.4. Procedure for determining the elective share.

(a) Exercisable Only During Lifetime. - The right of the surviving spouse to file a claim for an elective share must be exercised during the lifetime of the surviving spouse, by the surviving spouse, by the surviving spouse's attorney-in-fact if the surviving spouse's power of attorney expressly authorizes the attorney-in-fact to do so or to generally engage in estate transactions, or, with approval of court, by the guardian of the surviving spouse's estate or general guardian. If a surviving spouse dies before the claim for an elective share has been settled, the surviving spouse's personal representative shall succeed to the surviving spouse's rights to an elective share.

(b) Time Limitations. - A claim for an elective share must be made within six months after the issuance of letters testamentary or letters of administration in connection with the will or intestate proceeding with respect to which the surviving spouse claims the elective share by (i) filing a petition with the clerk of superior court of the county in which the primary administration of the decedent's estate lies, and (ii) mailing or delivering a copy of that petition to the personal representative of the decedent's estate. A surviving spouse's incapacity shall not toll the six-month period of limitations.

(c) Repealed by Session Laws 2011, c. 344, s. 6, effective January 1, 2012, and applicable to estates of decedents dying on or after that date.

(d) Repealed by Session Laws 2009, c. 368, s. 1, effective July 27, 2009, and applicable to decedents dying on or after October 1, 2009.

(d1) Mediation. - The clerk may order mediation as described in G.S. 7A-38.3B of any disputes in connection with an elective share proceeding.

(e) Repealed by Session Laws 2009, c. 368, s. 1, effective July 27, 2009, and applicable to decedents dying on or after October 1, 2009.

(e1) Procedure. - An elective share proceeding shall be an estate proceeding and shall be conducted in accordance with the procedures of Article 2 of Chapter 28A of the General Statutes.

(e2) Information About Total Net Assets. - In order to assist the clerk in determining whether a surviving spouse is entitled to an elective share, and, if so, the amount thereof, the following provisions apply:

(1) Submission within two months. - In every case in which a petition to determine an elective share has been filed, within two months of the filing of the petition, the personal representative shall submit sufficient information about the total assets for the clerk to determine the elective share. To fulfill its obligation to provide information, the personal representative may prepare and submit to the clerk a proposed Form 706, United States Estate (and Generation-Skipping Transfer) Tax Return, for the estate, regardless of whether that form is required to be filed with the Internal Revenue Service. The clerk may extend the time for submission of the proposed Form 706 or other information as the clerk sees fit.

(2) Examination regarding assets. - If the personal representative, the surviving spouse, or a responsible person has reasonable grounds to believe

that any person has a claim or has in its possession assets included in Total Net Assets, then the personal representative, surviving spouse, or responsible person may use the procedures set out in G.S. 28A-15-12 to cause the clerk to examine the person believed to have a claim or to possess assets included in Total Net Assets.

(f)   Findings and Conclusions. - After notice and hearing, the clerk shall determine whether or not the surviving spouse is entitled to an elective share, and if so, the clerk shall then determine the elective share and shall order the personal representative to transfer that amount to the surviving spouse. The clerk's order shall recite specific findings of fact and conclusions of law in arriving at the decedent's Total Net Assets, Property Passing to Surviving Spouse, and the elective share.

(g)   Repealed by Session Laws 2009, c. 368, s. 1, effective July 27, 2009, and applicable to decedents dying on or after October 1, 2009.

(h)   Expenses. - The expenses (including attorneys' fees) reasonably incurred by the personal representative, other responsible persons, and the surviving spouse in connection with elective share proceedings shall be equitably apportioned by the clerk of court in the clerk's discretion among the personal representative, other responsible persons, and the surviving spouse. (2000-178, s. 2; 2003-296, s. 4; 2009-368, s. 1; 2011-344, s. 6.)

§ 30-3.5. Satisfaction of elective share.

(a)   Repealed by Session Laws 2009, c. 368, s. 1, effective August 27, 2009, and applicable to decedents dying on or after October 1, 2009.

(a1)   Apportionment. - The personal representative shall apportion the liability to the surviving spouse for the amount of the elective share among all responsible persons as follows:

(1)   The net value of each nonspousal asset shall be determined by calculating the value of the nonspousal asset under G.S. 30-3.3A and reducing such value by that portion of the claims (including year's allowances to persons other than the surviving spouse) payable out of, charged against, or otherwise properly allocable to the nonspousal asset.

(2) Using the net value of each nonspousal asset as determined under subdivision (1) of this subsection, the personal representative shall determine each responsible person's liability to the surviving spouse by multiplying the amount of the elective share by a fraction, the numerator of which is the net value of the responsible person's nonspousal assets and the denominator of which is the net value of all of the nonspousal assets.

(a2) Recovery From Responsible Persons. - In recovering assets from responsible persons, the following rules apply:

(1) To the extent the personal representative is a responsible person, the personal representative shall satisfy its liability to the surviving spouse out of its nonspousal assets according to the following order of priority:

a. The personal representative shall satisfy its liability out of the net value of the nonspousal assets passing by intestate succession by allocating the liability proportionately among each intestate heir based on the fraction of the net value of the nonspousal assets passing by intestate succession that each intestate heir is entitled to receive.

b. If the net value of the nonspousal assets passing by intestate succession is not sufficient to satisfy the personal representative's liability in full, the personal representative shall satisfy its remaining liability out of the net value of the nonspousal assets passing as part of the decedent's residuary estate by allocating the liability proportionately among each beneficiary of the decedent's residuary estate based on the fraction of the net value of the nonspousal assets passing as part of the decedent's residuary estate that each residuary beneficiary is entitled to receive.

c. If the net value of the nonspousal assets in the residuary estate is not sufficient to satisfy the personal representative's liability in full, the personal representative shall satisfy its remaining liability by allocating the remaining liability proportionately among each other beneficiary of the decedent's will based on the fraction of the net value of the remaining nonspousal assets each other beneficiary is entitled to receive.

(2) The personal representative shall recover from each other responsible person the responsible person's liability to the surviving spouse.

(3) Each responsible person, including the personal representative in its capacity as a responsible person, may elect to satisfy its liability in full by any of the following methods:

a. Conveyance of that portion of the responsible person's nonspousal assets (or identical substitute assets), valued on the date of conveyance, sufficient to satisfy the responsible person's liability; or, if the value of the responsible person's nonspousal assets on the date of conveyance is less than the responsible person's liability, conveyance of all of the responsible person's nonspousal assets (or identical substitute assets).

b. Payment of the liability in cash.

c. Payment of the liability in other property upon written agreement of the surviving spouse at values agreed by the surviving spouse for purposes of determining the extent of the liability satisfied.

d. Any combination of the payment methods set forth under sub-subdivision a. through d. of this subdivision, provided that the total value of assets conveyed by the responsible person equals such responsible person's liability.

(a3) Inability or Refusal to Pay. - The personal representative shall be entitled to petition the clerk of court for an order requiring any responsible person to satisfy its liability. Upon refusal of a responsible person to obey such an order, the personal representative shall be entitled to a judgment against such responsible person in the amount of the liability and to any other remedies the clerk deems appropriate. Although the responsible person shall remain primarily liable for such responsible person's liability for the elective share, the following rules apply:

(1) If the responsible person makes a gratuitous transfer, whether inter vivos or by testate or intestate succession, of all or any part of the responsible person's nonspousal assets or the proceeds thereof after the decedent's death, then the gratuitous transferee shall be liable for the amount transferred, and the personal representative shall be entitled to recover that amount from the transferee as if the transferee were the responsible person.

(2) If the responsible person is a fiduciary and makes a distribution of all or any part of the responsible person's nonspousal assets or the proceeds thereof after the decedent's death, then the distributee shall be liable for the amount

transferred, and the personal representative shall be entitled to recover that amount from the distributee as if the distributee were the responsible person.

If, after exhausting all other remedies in this section, the personal representative cannot reasonably recover a responsible person's liability, then, with the approval of the clerk, the defaulting responsible person's liability shall be apportioned on a pro rata basis among the responsible persons who have not defaulted. Each nondefaulting other responsible person shall be liable for the amount of the liability apportioned to it in the same manner and to the same extent as its original liability for the elective share; provided, that each responsible person's liability shall not exceed the responsible person's proportionate share of the value of the nonspousal assets based on the values used in determining Total Net Assets. Each nondefaulting other responsible person shall be entitled to a proportionate share of any judgment against or subsequent recovery of the liability from the defaulting responsible person.

(b) Standstill Order. - After the filing of the petition demanding an elective share, the personal representative, surviving spouse, or any responsible person may request the clerk to issue an order that any responsible person not dispose of all or a portion of the decedent's Total Net Assets or the proceeds thereof pending the payment of the elective share. The decision to issue such an order shall be in the discretion of the clerk. A person who violates the standstill order may be held in civil contempt of court pursuant to Article 5A of Chapter 2 of the General Statutes. The clerk shall enter an order terminating the standstill order upon the clerk's determination that the standstill order is no longer necessary or desirable.

(c),(d) Repealed by Session Laws 2009, c. 368, s. 1, effective August 27, 2009, and applicable to decedents dying on or after October 1, 2009.

(e) Bond. - If a responsible person distributes or disposes of nonspousal assets prior to final apportionment of the elective share and expenses, the personal representative may require the responsible person or the transferee to provide a bond or other security for the responsible person's liability for payment of the elective share and apportioned expenses in the form and amount prescribed by the personal representative, with the approval of the clerk. (2000-178, s. 2; 2009-368, s. 1.)

§ 30-3.6. Waiver of rights.

(a) The right of a surviving spouse to claim an elective share may be waived, wholly or partially, before or after marriage, with or without consideration, by a written waiver signed by the surviving spouse, by the surviving spouse's attorney-in-fact if the surviving spouse's power of attorney expressly authorizes the attorney-in-fact to do so or to generally engage in estate transactions, or, with approval of court, by the guardian of the surviving spouse's estate or general guardian.

(b) A waiver is not enforceable if the surviving spouse proves that:

(1) The waiver was not executed voluntarily; or

(2) The surviving spouse or the surviving spouse's representative making the waiver was not provided a fair and reasonable disclosure of the property and financial obligations of the decedent, unless the surviving spouse waived, in writing, the right to that disclosure.

(c) A written waiver that would have been effective to waive a spouse's right to dissent in estates of decedents dying on or before December 31, 2000, under Article 1 of Chapter 30 of the General Statutes is effective to waive that spouse's right of elective share under this Article for estates of decedents dying on or after January 1, 2001. (2000-178, s. 2; 2003-296, s. 5; 2004-203, s. 30; 2009-368, s. 1.)

Article 2.

Dower.

§§ 30-4 through 30-8. Repealed by Session Laws 1959, c. 879, s. 14.

§ 30-9. Repealed by Session Laws 1965, c. 853.

§ 30-10. Repealed by Session Laws 1959, c. 879, s. 14.

Article 3.

Allotment of Dower.

§§ 30-11 through 30-14. Repealed by Session Laws 1959, c. 879, s. 14.

Article 4.

Year's Allowance.

Part 1. Nature of Allowance.

§ 30-15. When spouse entitled to allowance.

Every surviving spouse of an intestate or of a testator, whether or not the surviving spouse has petitioned for an elective share, shall, unless the surviving spouse has forfeited the surviving spouse's right thereto, as provided by law, be entitled, out of the personal property of the deceased spouse, to an allowance of the value of thirty thousand dollars ($30,000) for the surviving spouse's support for one year after the death of the deceased spouse. Such allowance shall be exempt from any lien, by judgment or execution, acquired against the property of the deceased spouse, and shall, in cases of testacy, be charged against the share of the surviving spouse. (1868-9, c. 93, s. 81; 1871-2, c. 193, s. 44; 1880, c. 42; Code, s. 2116; 1889, c. 499, s. 2; Rev., s. 3091; C.S., s. 4108; 1953, c. 913, s. 1; 1961, c. 316, s. 1; c. 749, s. 1; 1969, c. 14; 1981, c. 413, s. 1; 1995, c. 262, s. 4; 2000-178, s. 4; 2009-183, s. 1; 2011-344, s. 7; 2013-81, s. 1.)

§ 30-16. Duty of personal representative, magistrate, or clerk to assign allowance.

It shall be the duty of every administrator, collector, or executor of a will, on application in writing, signed by the surviving spouse, at any time within one year after the death of the deceased spouse, to assign to the surviving spouse the year's allowance as provided in this Article.

If there shall be no administration, or if the personal representative shall fail or refuse to apply to a magistrate or clerk of court, as provided in G.S. 30-20, for 10 days after the surviving spouse has filed the aforesaid application, or if the surviving spouse is the personal representative, the surviving spouse may make application to the magistrate or clerk, and it shall be the duty of the magistrate or clerk to proceed in the same manner as though the application had been made by the personal representative.

Where any personal property of the deceased spouse shall be located outside the township or county where the deceased spouse resided at the time of the deceased spouse's death, the personal representative or the surviving spouse may apply to any magistrate or to any clerk of court of any township or county where such personal property is located, and it shall be the duty of such magistrate or clerk to assign the year's allowance as if the deceased spouse had resided and died in that township. (1868-9, c. 93, s. 12; 1870-1, c. 263; Code, ss. 2120, 2122; 1889, cc. 496, 531; 1891, c. 13; Rev., ss. 3096, 3098; C.S., ss. 4113, 4115; 1961, c. 749, s. 2; 1971, c. 528, s. 21; 1997-310, s. 1; 2011-344, s. 7.)

§ 30-17. When children entitled to an allowance.

Whenever any parent dies survived by any child under the age of 18 years, including an adopted child or a child with whom the widow may be pregnant at the death of her husband, or a child who is less than 22 years of age and is a full-time student in any educational institution, or a child under 21 years of age who has been declared mentally incompetent, or a child under 21 years of age who is totally disabled, or any other person under the age of 18 years residing with the deceased parent at the time of death to whom the deceased parent or the surviving parent stood in loco parentis, every such child shall be entitled to receive an allowance of five thousand dollars ($5,000) for the child's support for the year next ensuing the death of the parent. The allowance shall be in addition to the child's share of the deceased parent's estate and shall be exempt from any lien by judgment or execution against the property of the deceased parent. The personal representative of the deceased parent shall, within one year after the parent's death, assign to every such child the allowance herein provided for; but if there is no personal representative or if the personal representative fails or refuses to act within 10 days after written application by a guardian or next friend on behalf of the child, the allowance may be assigned by a magistrate or clerk of court upon application.

If the child resides with the surviving spouse of the deceased parent at the time the allowance is paid, the allowance shall be paid to the surviving spouse for the benefit of the child. If the child resides with its surviving parent who is other than the surviving spouse of the deceased parent, the allowance shall be paid to the surviving parent for the use and benefit of the child. The payment shall be made regardless of whether the deceased died testate or intestate or whether the surviving spouse petitioned for an elective share under Article 1A of Chapter 30 of the General Statutes. Provided, however, the allowance shall not be available to a deceased father's child born out of wedlock, unless the deceased father has recognized the paternity of the child by deed, will, or other paper-writing, or unless the deceased father died prior to or within one year after the birth of the child and is established to have been the father of the child by DNA testing. If the child does not reside with a surviving spouse or a surviving parent when the allowance is paid, the allowance shall be paid to the child's general guardian, if any, and if none, to the clerk of the superior court who shall receive and disburse the allowance for the benefit of the child. (1889, c. 496; Rev., s. 3094; C.S., s. 4111; 1939, c. 396; 1953, c. 913, s. 2; 1961, c. 316, s. 2; c. 749, s. 3; 1969, c. 269; 1971, c. 528, s. 22; 1973, c. 1411; 1975, c. 259; 1981, c. 413, s. 2; c. 599, s. 7; 1995, c. 262, s. 5; 1997-310, s. 2; 2005-225, s. 1; 2011-344, s. 7; 2012-71, ss. 2(a), 3; 2013-198, s. 13.)

§ 30-18. From what property allowance assigned.

Such allowance shall be made in money or other personal property of the estate of the deceased spouse. (1868-9, c. 93, s. 9; Code, s. 2117; Rev., s. 3095; C.S., s. 4112; 1925, c. 92; 1961, c. 749, s. 4.)

Part 2. Assigned by Magistrate or Clerk.

§ 30-19. Value of property ascertained.

The value of the personal property assigned to the surviving spouse and children shall be ascertained by a magistrate or the clerk of court of the county in which administration was granted or the will probated. (1868-9, c. 93, s. 13; Code, s. 2121; Rev., s. 3097; C.S., s. 4114; 1961, c. 749, s. 5; 1971, c. 528, s. 22; 1989, c. 11, s. 1; 1997-310, s. 3.)

§ 30-20. Procedure for assignment.

Upon the application of the surviving spouse, a child by the child's guardian or next friend, or the personal representative of the deceased, the clerk of superior court of the county in which the deceased resided may assign the inquiry to a magistrate of the county. The clerk of court, or magistrate upon assignment, shall ascertain the person or persons entitled to an allowance according to the provisions of this Article, and determine the money or other personal property of the estate, and pay over to or assign to the surviving spouse and to the children, if any, so much thereof as they shall be entitled to as provided in this Article. Any deficiencies shall be made up from any of the personal property of the deceased, and if the personal property of the estate shall be insufficient to satisfy the allowance, the clerk of the superior court shall enter judgment against the personal representative for the amount of the deficiency, to be paid when a sufficiency of such assets shall come into the personal representative's hands. (1870-1, c. 263; Code, s. 2122; 1891, c. 13; 1899, c. 531; Rev., s. 3098; C.S., s. 4115; 1961, c. 749, s. 6; 1971, c. 528, s. 23; 1989, c. 11, s. 2; 1997-310, s. 3; 2011-344, s. 7; 2012-71, s. 2(b).)

§ 30-21. Report of clerk or magistrate.

The clerk of court, or magistrate upon assignment, shall make and sign three lists of the money or other personal property assigned to each person, stating their quantity and value, and the deficiency to be paid by the personal representative. Where the allowance is to the surviving spouse, one of these lists shall be delivered to the surviving spouse. Where the allowance is to a child, one of these lists shall be delivered to the surviving parent with whom the child is living; or to the child's guardian or next friend if the child is not living with the surviving parent; or to the child if the child is not living with the surviving parent and has no guardian or next friend. One list shall be delivered to the personal representative. One list shall be returned by the magistrate or clerk, within 20 days after the assignment, to the superior court of the county in which administration was granted or the will probated, and the clerk shall file and record the list, together with any judgment entered pursuant to G.S. 30-20. (1868-9, c. 93, s. 15; Code, s. 2123; Rev., s. 3099; C.S., s. 4116; 1961, c. 749, s. 7; 1971, c. 528, s. 24; 1989, c. 11, s. 3; 1997-310, s. 3; 2011-344, s. 7; 2012-71, s. 2(c).)

§ 30-22. Repealed by Session Laws 1971, c. 528, s. 25.

§ 30-23. Right of appeal.

The personal representative, or the surviving spouse, or child by a the child's guardian or next friend, or any creditor, devisee, or heir of the deceased, may appeal from the finding of the magistrate or clerk of court to the superior court of the county, by filing a copy of the assignment and a notice of appeal within 10 days after the assignment, and the appeal shall be heard as provided in G.S. 1-301.2, provided that the hearing on the appeal shall be at the next available session of superior court. (1868-9, c. 93, s. 16; Code, s. 2124; 1897, c. 442; Rev., s. 3100; C.S., s. 4117; 1961, c. 749, s. 9; 1989, c. 11, s. 4; 1997-310, s. 3; 2011-284, s. 23; 2011-344, s. 7; 2012-71, s. 2(d).)

§ 30-24: Repealed by Session Laws 2011-344, s. 7, effective January 1, 2012, and applicable to estates of decedents dying on or after that date.

§ 30-25. Personal representative entitled to credit.

Upon the settlement of the accounts of the personal representative, the personal representative shall be credited with the articles assigned, and the value of the deficiency assessed as aforesaid, if the same shall have been paid, unless the allowance be impeached for fraud or gross negligence in him. (1868-9, c. 93, s. 18; Code, s. 2126; Rev., s. 3102; C.S., s. 4119; 1997, c. 310, s. 3; 2011-344, s. 7.)

§ 30-26: Repealed by Session Laws 2011-344, s. 7, effective January 1, 2012, and applicable to estates of decedents dying on or after that date.

Part 3. Assigned in Superior Court.

§ 30-27. Surviving spouse or child may apply to superior court.

In addition to any support otherwise assigned to the surviving spouse or child under this Article, without application to the personal representative, the surviving spouse, or the child through the child's guardian or next friend may, after the date specified in the general notice to creditors as provided for in G.S. 28A-14-1(a), and within one year after the decedent's death, apply to the superior court of the county in which administration was granted or the will probated to have a year's support assigned at an amount other than prescribed in G.S. 30-15 and G.S. 30-17. (1868-9, c. 93, s. 20; Code, s. 2128; Rev., s. 3104; C.S., s. 4121; 1961, c. 749, s. 11; 2011-344, s. 7; 2012-71, s. 2(e).)

§ 30-28. Nature of proceeding; parties.

The application shall be by petition in a special proceeding before the clerk of superior court. The personal representative of the deceased, if there is one other than the petitioner, all known creditors, and all known heirs of the deceased, if the deceased is intestate, and devisees of the deceased, if the deceased is testate, shall be made parties to the special proceeding. If the personal representative of the deceased is aware of a creditor, heir, or devisee who should have been made a respondent but was not, then the personal representative shall file a motion to add the creditor, heir, or devisee as a necessary party, and the court shall order such other party to appear in the proceeding. (1868-9, c. 93, s. 21; Code, s. 2129; Rev., s. 3105; C.S., s. 4122; 2011-284, s. 24; 2011-344, s. 7.)

§ 30-29. What petition must show.

In the petition the petitioner shall set forth, besides the facts entitling petitioner to a year's support and the value of the support claimed, the further facts that the personal estate of which the decedent died possessed exceeded thirty thousand dollars ($30,000), and also whether or not an allowance has been made to petitioner and the nature and value thereof. (1868-9, c. 93, s. 22; Code, s. 2130; Rev., s. 3106; C.S., s. 4123; 1961, c. 749, s. 12; 1981, c. 413, s. 4; 1995, c. 262, s. 7; 2009-183, s. 3; 2011-344, s. 7; 2013-81, s. 2.)

§ 30-30. Judgment.

The clerk of superior court shall hear the matter and determine whether the petitioner is entitled to some or all of the relief sought and, if the clerk determines that the petitioner is so entitled, the clerk shall determine the money or other personal property of the estate and assign to the petitioner a sufficiency thereof for petitioner's support for one year from the decedent's death. Any deficiency shall be made up from any of the personal property of the deceased, and if the personal property of the estate shall be insufficient for such support, the clerk of superior court shall enter judgment against the personal representative for the amount of such deficiency, to be paid when a sufficiency of such assets shall come into the personal representative's hands. Any judgment so rendered shall have the same priority over other debts and claims against the estate as an allowance assigned pursuant to G.S. 30-15 or G.S. 30-17. (1868-9, c. 93, s. 23; Code, s. 2131; Rev., s. 3107; C.S., s. 4124; 1961, c. 749, s. 13; 1971, c. 528, s. 26; 2011-344, s. 7; 2012-194, s. 14.)

§ 30-31. Amount of allowance.

The clerk of superior court may assign to the petitioner a value sufficient for the support of petitioner according to the estate and condition of the decedent and without regard to the limitations set forth in this Chapter; but the value allowed shall be fixed with due consideration for other persons entitled to allowances for year's support from the decedent's estate; and the total value of all allowances shall not in any case exceed the one half of the average annual net income of the deceased for three years next preceding the deceased's death. Attorneys' fees and costs awarded the petitioner under G.S. 6-21 shall be paid as an administrative expense of the estate. (1868-9, c. 93, s. 24; Code, s. 2132; Rev., s. 3108; C.S., s. 4125; 1971, c. 528, s. 27; 2011-344, s. 7; 2012-18, s. 3.10; 2013-91, s. 1(e).)

§ 30-31.1. Service of judgment and appeal.

The petitioner shall serve the clerk's judgment on all other parties. The judgment also shall be filed in the estate file of the deceased. Any aggrieved party may appeal the judgment in accordance with G.S. 1-301.2. (2011-344, s. 7.)

§ 30-31.2. Execution.

If the clerk's judgment is not appealed as provided in G.S. 1-301.2, execution shall issue to enforce the judgment as in like cases under Article 28 of Chapter 1 of the General Statutes. (2011-344, s. 7.)

§ 30-32: Repealed by Session Laws 2012-194, s. 40, effective July 17, 2012.

§ 30-33: Repealed by Session Laws 2011-344, s. 7, effective January 1, 2012, and applicable to estates of decedents dying on or after that date.

Chapter 31.

Wills.

Article 1.

Execution of Will.

§ 31-1. Who may make will.

Any person of sound mind, and 18 years of age or over, may make a will. (1811, c. 280; R.C., c. 119, s. 2; Code, s. 2137; Rev., s. 3111; C.S., s. 4128; 1953, c. 1098, s. 1; 1965, c. 303; 1969, c. 39.)

§ 31-2. Repealed by Session Laws 1953, c. 1098, s. 1.

§ 31-3: Rewritten and renumbered as G.S. 31-3.1 to 31-3.6 by Session Laws 1953, c. 1098, s. 2.

§ 31-3.1. Will invalid unless statutory requirements complied with.

No will is valid unless it complies with the requirements prescribed therefor by this Article. (1953, c. 1098, s. 2.)

§ 31-3.2. Kinds of wills.

(a) Personal property and real property may be devised by

(1) An attested written will which complies with the requirements of G.S. 31-3.3, or

(2) A holographic will which complies with the requirements of G.S. 31-3.4.

(b) Personal property may also be devised by a nuncupative will which complies with the requirements of G.S. 31-3.5. (1953, c. 1098, s. 2; 2011-284, s. 26.)

§ 31-3.3. Attested written will.

(a) An attested written will is a written will signed by the testator and attested by at least two competent witnesses as provided by this section.

(b) The testator must, with intent to sign the will, do so by actually signing the will or by having someone else in the testator's presence and at the testator's direction sign the testator's name thereon.

(c) The testator must signify to the attesting witnesses that the instrument is the testator's instrument by signing it in their presence or by acknowledging to them the testator's signature previously affixed thereto, either of which may be done before the attesting witnesses separately.

(d) The attesting witnesses must sign the will in the presence of the testator but need not sign in the presence of each other. (1953, c. 1098, s. 2; 2011-344, s. 8.)

§ 31-3.4. Holographic will.

(a) A holographic will is a will

(1) Written entirely in the handwriting of the testator but when all the words appearing on a paper in the handwriting of the testator are sufficient to constitute a valid holographic will, the fact that other words or printed matter appear thereon not in the handwriting of the testator, and not affecting the meaning of the words in such handwriting, shall not affect the validity of the will, and

(2) Subscribed by the testator, or with the testator's name written in or on the will in the testator's own handwriting, and

(3) Found after the testator's death among the testator's valuable papers or effects, or in a safe-deposit box or other safe place where it was deposited by the testator or under the testator's authority, or in the possession or custody of some person with whom, or some firm or corporation with which, it was deposited by the testator or under the testator's authority for safekeeping.

(b) No attesting witness to a holographic will is required. (1953, c. 1098, s. 2; 1955, c. 73, s. 1; 2011-344, s. 8.)

§ 31-3.5. Nuncupative will.

A nuncupative will is a will

(1) Made orally by a person who is in that person's last sickness or in imminent peril of death and who does not survive such sickness or imminent peril, and

(2) Declared to be that person's will before two competent witnesses simultaneously present at the making thereof and specially requested by the person to bear witness thereto. (1953, c. 1098, s. 2; 2011-344, s. 8.)

§ 31-3.6. Seal not required.

A seal is not necessary to the validity of a will. (1953, c. 1098, s. 2.)

§ 31-4. Execution of power of appointment by will.

No appointment, made by will in the exercise of any power, shall be valid unless the same be executed in the manner by law required for the execution of wills; and every will, executed in such manner, shall, so far as respects the execution and attestation thereof, be a valid execution of a power of appointment by will, notwithstanding it shall have been expressly required that a will made in exercise of such power should be executed with some additional or other form of execution or solemnity. (1844, c. 88, s. 9; R.C., c. 119, s. 4; Code, s. 2139; Rev., s. 3114; C.S., s. 4132.)

§ 31-4.1: Repealed by Session Laws 2010-181, s. 1, effective July 1, 2010.

§ 31-4.2: Repealed by Session Laws 2010-181, s. 2, effective July 1, 2010.

Article 2.

Revocation of Will.

§ 31-5: Rewritten and renumbered as G.S. 31-5.1 by Session Laws 1953, c. 1098, s. 3.

§ 31-5.1. Revocation of written will.

A written will, or any part thereof, may be revoked only

(1) By a subsequent written will or codicil or other revocatory writing executed in the manner provided herein for the execution of written wills, or

(2) By being burnt, torn, canceled, obliterated, or destroyed, with the intent and for the purpose of revoking it, by the testator himself or by another person in the testator's presence and by the testator's direction. (1784, c. 204, s. 14; 1819, c. 1004, ss. 1, 2; 1840, c. 62; R.C., c. 119, s. 22; Code, s. 2176; Rev., s. 3115; C.S., s. 4133; 1945, c. 140; 1953, c. 1098, s. 3; 2011-344, s. 8.)

§ 31-5.2. Revocation of nuncupative will.

A nuncupative will or any part thereof may be revoked

(1) By a subsequent nuncupative will, or

(2) By a subsequent written will or codicil or other revocatory writing executed in the manner provided herein for the execution of written wills. (1953, c. 1098, s. 4.)

§ 31-5.3. Will not revoked by marriage; dissent from will made prior to marriage.

A will is not revoked by a subsequent marriage of the maker; and the surviving spouse may petition for an elective share when there is a will made prior to the marriage in the same manner, upon the same conditions, and to the same extent, as a surviving spouse may petition for an elective share when there is a will made subsequent to marriage. (1844, c. 88, s. 10; R.C., c. 119, s. 23; Code, s. 2177; Rev., s. 3116; C.S., s. 4134; 1947, c. 110; 1953, c. 1098, s. 5; 1967, c. 128; 2000-178, s. 5.)

§ 31-5.4. Revocation by divorce or annulment; revival.

Dissolution of marriage by absolute divorce or annulment after making a will does not revoke the will of any testator but, unless otherwise specifically provided in the will, it revokes all provisions in the will in favor of the testator's former spouse or purported former spouse, including, but not by way of limitation, any provision conferring a general or special power of appointment on the former spouse or purported former spouse and any appointment of the former spouse or purported former spouse as executor, trustee, conservator, or guardian. If provisions are revoked solely by this section, they are revived by the testator's remarriage to the former spouse or purported former spouse. (1953, c. 1098, s. 6; 1977, c. 74, s. 3; 1991, c. 587, s. 1.)

§ 31-5.5. After-born or after-adopted child; children born out of wedlock; effect on will.

(a)   A will shall not be revoked by the subsequent birth of a child to the testator, or by the subsequent adoption of a child by the testator, or by the subsequent entitlement of an after-born child born out of wedlock to take as an heir of the testator pursuant to the provisions of G.S. 29-19(b), but any after-born, after-adopted or entitled after-born child born out of wedlock shall have the right to share in the testator's estate to the same extent the after-born, after-adopted, or entitled after-born child born out of wedlock would have shared if the testator had died intestate unless:

(1)   The testator made some provision in the will for the child, whether adequate or not;

(2)   It is apparent from the will itself that the testator intentionally did not make specific provision therein for the child;

(3)   The testator had children living when the will was executed, and none of the testator's children actually take under the will;

(4)   The surviving spouse receives all of the estate under the will; or

(5) The testator made provision for the child that takes effect upon the death of the testator, whether adequate or not.

(b) The provisions of G.S. 28A-22-2 shall be construed as being applicable to after-adopted children and to after-born children, whether legitimate or entitled children born out of wedlock.

(c) The terms "after-born," "after-adopted" and "entitled after-born" as used in this section refer to children born, adopted or entitled subsequent to the execution of the will. (1868-9, c. 113, s. 62; Code, s. 2145; Rev., s. 3145; C.S., s. 4169; 1953, c. 1098, s. 7; 1955, c. 541; 1973, c. 1062, s. 2; 1985, c. 689, s. 9; 1995, c. 161, s. 1; 1997-456, s. 55.8; 2011-344, s. 8; 2013-198, s. 14.)

§ 31-5.6. No revocation by subsequent conveyance.

No conveyance or other act made or done subsequently to the execution of a will of, or relating to, any real or personal estate therein comprised, except an act by which such will shall be duly revoked, shall prevent the operation of the will with respect to any estate or interest in such real or personal estate as the testator shall have power to dispose of by will at the time of the testator's death. (1844, c. 88, s. 2; R.C. c. 119, s. 25; Code, s. 2179; Rev., s. 3118; C.S., s. 4136; 1953, c. 1098, s. 8; 2011-344, s. 8.)

§ 31-5.7. Specific provisions for revocation exclusive; effect of changes in circumstances.

No will can be revoked in whole or in part by any act of the testator or by a change in the testator's circumstances or condition except as provided by G.S. 31-5.1 through 31-5.6 inclusive. (1953, c. 1098, s. 9; 2011-344, s. 8.)

§ 31-5.8. Revival of revoked will.

No will or any part thereof that has been in any manner revoked can, except as provided in G.S. 31-5.4, be revived otherwise than by a reexecution thereof, or by the execution of another will in which the revoked will or part thereof is incorporated by reference. (1953, c. 1098, s. 10; 1991, c. 587, s. 2.)

§ 31-6: Renumbered as G.S. 31-5.3 by Session Laws 1953, c. 1098, s. 5.

§ 31-7. Repealed by Session Laws 1953, c. 1098, s. 9.

§ 31-8: Renumbered as G.S. 31-5.6 by Session Laws 1953, c. 1098, s. 8.

Article 3.

Witnesses to Will.

§ 31-8.1. Who may witness.

Any person competent to be a witness generally in this State may act as a witness to a will. (1953, c. 1098, s. 15.)

§ 31-9. Executor competent witness.

No person, on account of being an executor of a will, shall be incompetent to be admitted a witness to prove the execution of such will, or to prove the validity or invalidity thereof. (R.C., c. 119, s. 9; Code, s. 2146; Rev., s. 3119; C.S., s. 4137.)

§ 31-10. Beneficiary competent witness; when interest rendered void.

(a) A witness to an attested written or a nuncupative will, to whom or to whose spouse a beneficial interest in property, or a power of appointment with respect thereto, is given by the will, is nevertheless a competent witness to the will and is competent to prove the execution or validity thereof. However, if there are not at least two other witnesses to the will who are disinterested, the interested witness and the interested witness's spouse and anyone claiming under the interested witness shall take nothing under the will, and so far only as their interests are concerned the will is void.

(b) A beneficiary under a holographic will may testify to such competent, relevant and material facts as tend to establish such holographic will as a valid will without rendering void the benefits to be received by the beneficiary thereunder. (R.C., c. 119, s. 10; Code, s. 2147; Rev., s. 3120; C.S., s. 4138; 1953, c. 1098, s. 11; 1955, c. 73, s. 2; 2011-344, s. 8.)

§ 31-10.1. Corporate trustee not disqualified by witnessing of will by stockholder.

A corporation named as a trustee in a will is not disqualified to act as trustee by reason of the fact that a person owning stock in the corporation signed the will as a witness. (1949, c. 44.)

Article 4.

Depository for Wills.

§ 31-11. Depositories in offices of clerks of superior court where living persons may file wills.

The clerk of the superior court in each county of North Carolina shall be required to keep a receptacle or depository in which any person who desires to do so may file that person's will for safekeeping; and the clerk shall, upon written request of the testator, or the duly authorized agent or attorney for the testator, permit said will or testament to be withdrawn from said depository or receptacle at any time prior to the death of the testator: Provided, that the contents of said will shall not be made public or open to the inspection of anyone other than the testator or the testator's duly authorized agent until such time as the said will shall be offered for probate. (1937, c. 435, s. 1; 1971, c. 528, s. 28; 2011-344, s. 8.)

§§ 31-11.1 through 31-11.5. Reserved for future codification purposes.

Article 4A.

Self-Proved Wills.

§ 31-11.6. How attested wills may be made self-proved.

(a) Any will may be simultaneously executed, attested, and made self-proved, by acknowledgment thereof by the testator and affidavits of the witnesses, each made before an officer authorized to administer oaths under the laws of the state where execution occurs and evidenced by the officer's certificate, under official seal, in the following form, or in a similar form showing the same intent:

"I, _____, the testator, sign my name to this instrument this ____ day of _____, ____ and being first duly sworn, do hereby declare to the undersigned authority that I sign and execute this instrument as my last will and that I sign it willingly (or willingly direct another to sign for me), that I execute it as my free and voluntary act for the purposes therein expressed, and that I am eighteen years of age or older, of sound mind, and under no constraint or undue influence.

_____

Testator

We _____, _____, the witnesses, sign our names to this instrument, being first duly sworn, and do hereby declare to the undersigned authority that the testator signs and executes this instrument as his last will and that he signs it willingly (or willingly directs another to sign for him), and that each of us, in the presence and hearing of the testator, hereby signs this will as witness to the testator's signing, and to the best of our knowledge the testator is eighteen years of age or older, of sound mind, and under no constraint or undue influence.

_____

Witness

_____

Witness

THE STATE OF _____.

COUNTY OF _____.

Subscribed, sworn to and acknowledged before me by _____. the testator and subscribed and sworn to before me by _____ and _____, witnesses, this ____ day of _____

(SEAL)

(SIGNED) _____

(OFFICIAL CAPACITY OF OFFICER)"

(b)   An attested written will executed as provided by G.S. 31-3.3 may at any time subsequent to its execution be made self-proved, by the acknowledgment thereof by the testator and the affidavits of the attesting witnesses, each made before an officer authorized to administer oaths under the laws of this State, and evidenced by the officer's certificate, under official seal, attached or annexed to the will in form and content substantially as follows:

"STATE OF NORTH CAROLINA

"COUNTY/CITY OF _____

"Before me, the undersigned authority, on this day personally appeared _____, and _____, known to me to be the testator and the witnesses, respectively, whose names are signed to the attached or foregoing instrument and, all of these persons being by me first duly sworn. The testator, declared to me and to the witnesses in my presence: That said instrument is his last will; that he had willingly signed or directed another to sign the same for him, and executed it in the presence of said witnesses as his free and voluntary act for the purposes therein expressed; or, that the testator signified that the instrument was his instrument by acknowledging to them his signature previously affixed thereto.

The said witnesses stated before me that the foregoing will was executed and acknowledged by the testator as his last will in the presence of said witnesses who, in his presence and at his request, subscribed their names thereto as attesting witnesses and that the testator, at the time of the execution of said will, was over the age of 18 years and of sound and disposing mind and memory.

_____
Testator

_____
Witness

_____
Witness

_____
Witness

Subscribed, sworn and acknowledged before me by _____, the testator, subscribed and sworn before me by _____, _____ and _____ witnesses, this ____ day of _____, A.D. ____

(SEAL)

(SIGNED) _____

(OFFICIAL CAPACITY OF OFFICER)"

(c) The sworn statement of any such witnesses taken as herein provided shall be accepted by the court as if it had been taken before such court.

(d) Any will executed in another state and shown by the propounder to have been made self-proved under the laws of that state shall be considered as self-proved.

(e) A military testamentary instrument executed in accordance with the provisions of 10 U.S.C. § 1044d(d) or any successor or replacement statute shall be considered as self-proved. (1977, c. 795, s. 1; 1979, c. 536, s. 1; 1981, c. 599, s. 8; 1999-456, s. 59; 2013-91, s. 1(f).)

Article 5.

Probate of Will.

§§ 31-12 through 31-31.2: Recodified as Article 2A of Chapter 28A of the General Statutes, G.S. 28A-2A-1 through G.S. 28A-2A-23, by Session Laws 2011-344, s. 3, effective January 1, 2012, and applicable to estates of decedents dying on or after that date.

§ 31-18: §§ 31-12 through 31-31.2: Recodified as Article 2A of Chapter 28A of the General Statutes, G.S. 28A-2A-1 through G.S. 28A-2A-23, by Session Laws 2011-344, s. 3, effective January 1, 2012, and applicable to estates of decedents dying on or after that date.

§§ 31-12 through 31-31.2: Recodified as Article 2A of Chapter 28A of the General Statutes, G.S. 28A-2A-1 through G.S. 28A-2A-23, by Session Laws 2011-344, s. 3, effective January 1, 2012, and applicable to estates of decedents dying on or after that date.

§§ 31-25 through 31-25.1: Recodified as Article 2A of Chapter 28A of the General Statutes, G.S. 28A-2A-1 through G.S. 28A-2A-23, by Session Laws 2011-344, s. 3, effective January 1, 2012, and applicable to estates of decedents dying on or after that date.

§ 31-26: Recodified as Article 2A of Chapter 28A of the General Statutes, G.S. 28A-2A-1 through G.S. 28A-2A-23, by Session Laws 2011-344, s. 3, effective January 1, 2012, and applicable to estates of decedents dying on or after that date.

§§ 31-12 through 31-31.2: Recodified as Article 2A of Chapter 28A of the General Statutes, G.S. 28A-2A-1 through G.S. 28A-2A-23, by Session Laws 2011-344, s. 3, effective January 1, 2012, and applicable to estates of decedents dying on or after that date.

Article 6.

Caveat to Will.

§ 31-32. Filing of caveat.

(a) At the time of application for probate of any will, and the probate thereof in common form, or at any time within three years thereafter, any party interested in the estate, may appear in person or by attorney before the clerk of the superior court and enter a caveat to the probate of such will; Provided that if any person entitled to file a caveat be within the age of 18 years, or incompetent as defined in G.S. 35A-1101(7) or (8), then such person may file a caveat within three years after the removal of such disability.

(b) The caveat shall be filed in the decedent's estate file. The clerk of superior court shall give notice of the filing by making an entry upon the page of the will book where the will is recorded, evidencing that the caveat has been filed and giving the date of such filing.

(c) If a will has been probated in solemn form pursuant to G.S. 28A-2A-7, any party who was properly served in that probate in solemn form shall be barred from filing a caveat. (C.C.P., s. 446; Code, s. 2158; Rev., s. 3135; 1907, c. 862; C.S., s. 4158; 1925, c. 81; 1951, c. 496, ss. 1, 2; 1971, c. 1231, s. 1; 2011-344, s. 8.)

§ 31-33. Cause transferred to trial docket.

The caveator's

(a) Upon the filing of a caveat, the clerk shall transfer the cause to the superior court for trial by jury. The caveat shall be served upon all interested parties in accordance with G.S. 1A-1, Rule 4 of the Rules of Civil Procedure.

(b) After service under subsection (a) of this section, the caveator shall cause notice of a hearing to align the parties to be served upon all parties in accordance with G.S. 1A-1, Rule 5 of the Rules of Civil Procedure. At the alignment hearing, all of the interested parties who wish to be aligned as parties shall appear and be aligned by the court as parties with the caveators or parties with the propounders of the will. If an interested party does not appear to be aligned or chooses not to be aligned, the judge shall dismiss that interested party from the proceeding, but that party shall be bound by the proceeding.

(c) Within 30 days following the entry of an order aligning the parties, any interested party who was aligned may file a responsive pleading to the caveat, provided, however, that failure to respond to any averment or claim of the caveat shall not be deemed an admission of that averment or claim. An extension of time to file a responsive pleading to the caveat may be granted as provided by G.S. 1A-1, Rule 6 of the Rules of Civil Procedure.

(d) Upon motion of an aligned party, the court may require a caveator to provide security in such sum as the court deems proper for the payment of such costs and damages as may be incurred or suffered by the estate if the estate is found to have been wrongfully enjoined or restrained. The court may consider relevant facts related to whether a bond should be required and the amount of any such bond, including, but not limited to, (i) whether the estate may suffer irreparable injury, loss, or damage as a result of the caveat and (ii) whether the caveat has substantial merit. Provisions for bringing suit in forma pauperis apply to the provisions of this subsection. (C.C.P., s. 447; Code, s. 2159; 1899, c. 13; 1901, c. 748; Rev., s. 3136; 1909, c. 74; C.S., s. 4159; 1947, c. 781; 1971, c. 528, s. 29; 1973, c. 458; 2011-284, s. 32; 2011-344, s. 8.)

§ 31-34: Repealed by Session Laws 2011-344, s. 8, effective January 1, 2012, and applicable to estates of decedents dying on or after that date.

§ 31-35. Affidavit of witness as evidence.

Whenever the subscribing witness to any will shall die, or be mentally incompetent, or be absent beyond the State, it shall be competent upon any issue of devisavit vel non to give in evidence the affidavits and proofs taken by the clerk upon admitting the will to probate in common form, and such affidavit and proceedings before the clerk shall be prima facie evidence of the due and legal execution of said will. (1899, c. 680, s. 2; Rev., s. 3121; C.S., s. 4160; 1947, c. 781; 2011-344, s. 8.)

§ 31-36. Effect of caveat on estate administration.

(a) Order of Clerk. - Where a caveat is filed, the clerk of the superior court shall forthwith issue an order that shall apply during the pendency of the caveat to any personal representative, having the estate in charge, as follows:

(1) Distributions to beneficiaries. - That there shall be no distributions of assets of the estate to any beneficiary;

(2) Commissions. - That no commissions shall be advanced or awarded to any personal representative;

(3) Accountings. - That the personal representative shall file all accountings required by the clerk of superior court and that the personal representative may pay any applicable filing fees associated with those accountings from the assets of the estate;

(4) Preservation of estate assets. - That the personal representative shall preserve the property of the estate and that the personal representative is authorized to pursue and prosecute claims that the estate may have against others; and

(5) Taxes, claims and debts of estate. - That the personal representative may file all appropriate tax returns and that the personal representative may pay, in accordance with the procedures of subsection (b) of this section: taxes; funeral expenses of the decedent; debts that are a lien upon the property of the decedent; bills of the decedent accrued before death; claims against the estate that are timely filed; professional fees related to administration of the estate, including fees for tax return preparation, appraisal fees, and attorneys' fees for estate administration.

(b) Procedures. - In regard to payment of any of the items listed in subdivision (5) of subsection (a) of this section, the personal representative shall file with the clerk a notice of the personal representative's intent to pay those items and shall serve the notice upon all parties to the caveat, pursuant to G.S. 1A-1, Rule 4 of the Rules of Civil Procedure. If within 10 days of service any party files with the clerk a written objection to that payment, the clerk shall schedule a hearing and determine whether the proposed payment shall be made. If no such objection is filed with the clerk, the clerk may approve the payment without hearing, and upon that approval, the personal representative may make the payment. The parties to the caveat may consent to any such payment, and upon such consent, the clerk may approve the payment without hearing. The clerk may defer ruling on the payment pending the resolution of the caveat.

(c) Preservation of Estate Assets. - Questions regarding the use, location, and disposition of assets that cannot be resolved by the parties and consented to by the clerk shall be decided by the clerk. When a question has not been resolved by agreement, either party may request a hearing before the clerk upon 10 days notice and shall serve the notice upon all parties to the caveat, pursuant to G.S. 1A-1, Rule 4 of the Rules of Civil Procedure. Decisions of the clerk may be appealed to the superior court pursuant to G.S. 1-301.3. (C.C.P., s. 448; Code, s. 2160; Rev., s. 3137; C.S., s. 4161; 1927, c. 119; 2009-131, s. 1; 2011-344, s. 8.)

§ 31-37: Repealed by Session Laws 2011-344, s. 8, effective January 1, 2012, and applicable to estates of decedents dying on or after that date.

§ 31-37.1. Settlement agreement; filing of judgment.

(a) Prior to an entry of judgment by the superior court in a caveat proceeding, the parties may enter into a settlement agreement, which must be approved by the superior court. Upon approval of a settlement agreement, the court shall enter judgment, without a verdict by a jury, in accordance with the terms of the settlement agreement. The consent of interested parties who are not aligned as parties pursuant to G.S. 31-33 is not necessary for a settlement agreement under this section.

(b) When judgment is entered by the superior court in a caveat proceeding, the clerk of superior court shall file a copy of the judgment in the estate file and shall make entry upon the page of the will book where such will is recorded to the effect that final judgment has been entered, either sustaining or setting aside the will. (1989 (Reg. Sess., 1990), c. 949, s. 1; 2011-344, s. 8.)

Article 7.

Construction of Will.

§ 31-38. Devise presumed to be in fee.

When real estate shall be devised to any person, the same shall be held and construed to be a devise in fee simple, unless such devise shall, in plain and express words, show, or it shall be plainly intended by the will, or some part thereof, that the testator intended to convey an estate of less dignity. (1784, c. 204, s. 12; R.C., c. 119, s. 26; Code, s. 2180; Rev., s. 3138; C.S., s. 4162.)

§ 31-39. Probate necessary to pass title; rights of lien creditors and purchasers; recordation in county where real property lies.

(a) A duly probated will is effective to pass title to real and personal property.

(b) A will is not effective to pass title to real or personal property as against lien creditors or purchasers for valuable consideration from the intestate heirs at law of a decedent, unless the will is probated or offered for probate before the earlier of (i) the date of the approval by the clerk of the superior court having jurisdiction of the decedent's estate of the final account filed by the personal representative of the decedent's estate, or (ii) the date that is two years from the date of death of the decedent. If the will is fraudulently suppressed, stolen, or destroyed, or is lost, and an action or proceeding is instituted within the time limitation set forth in this subsection to obtain that will or establish that will as provided by law, the time limitation under this subsection begins to run from the termination of that action or proceeding.

(c) A will duly probated in one county of this State is not effective to pass title to an interest in real property located in any other county of this State as against lien creditors or purchasers for valuable consideration from the intestate heirs at law of a decedent unless a certified copy of the will is filed in the office of the clerk of superior court in the county where the real property lies within the time limitation set forth in subsection (b) of this section.

(d) A conveyance made by the intestate heirs at law of a decedent before the expiration of the time limitation set forth in subsection (b) of this section shall, upon the expiration of that time, become effective to the same extent as if the conveyance were made after the expiration of that time, unless before the expiration of that time, a proceeding is instituted in the proper court to probate a will of the decedent. (1784, c. 225, s. 6; R.C., c. 119, s. 20; Code, s. 2174; Rev., s. 3139; 1915, c. 219; C.S., s. 4163; 1953, c. 920, s. 1; 2012-68, s. 2.)

§ 31-40. What property passes by will.

Any testator, by the testator's a will duly executed, may devise or dispose of all real and personal property which the testator shall be entitled to at the time of the testator's death, and which, if not so devised or disposed of, would descend or devolve upon the testator's heirs at law, or upon the testator's personal representative; and the power hereby given shall extend to all contingent, executory, or other future interest in any real or personal property, whether the testator may or may not be the person or one of the persons in whom the same may become vested, or whether the testator may be entitled thereto under the instrument by which the same was created, or under any disposition thereof by deed or will; and also to all rights of entry for conditions broken, whether any such condition has or has not been broken at the testator's death, all other rights of entry, and possibilities of reverter; and also to such of the same estates, interests, and rights respectively, and other real and personal property, as the testator may be entitled to at the time of the testator's death, notwithstanding that the testator may become entitled to the same subsequently to the execution of the testator's will. (1844, c. 88, s. 1; R.C., c. 119, s. 5; Code, s. 2140; Rev., s. 3140; C.S., s. 4164; 1973, c. 1446, s. 15; 2011-284, s. 33; 2011-344, s. 8.)

§ 31-41. Will relates to death of testator.

Every will shall be construed, with reference to the real and personal estate comprised therein, to speak and take effect as if it had been executed immediately before the death of the testator, unless a contrary intention shall appear by the will. (1844, c. 88, s. 3; R.C., c. 119, s. 16; Code, s. 2141; Rev., s. 3141; C.S., s. 4165.)

§ 31-42. Failure of devises by lapse or otherwise; renunciation; 120-hour survivorship requirement, revised simultaneous death act, Article 24, Chapter 28A.

(a) Unless the will indicates a contrary intent, if a devisee predeceases the testator, whether before or after the execution of the will, and if the devisee is a grandparent of or a descendant of a grandparent of the testator, then the issue of the predeceased devisee shall take in place of the deceased devisee. The devisee's issue shall take the deceased devisee's share in the same manner that the issue would take as heirs of the deceased devisee under the intestacy provisions in effect at the time of the testator's death. The provisions of this section apply whether the devise is to an individual, to a class, or is a residuary devise. In the case of the class devise, the issue shall take whatever share the deceased devisee would have taken had the devisee survived the testator; in the event the deceased class member leaves no issue, the devisee's share shall devolve upon the members of the class who survived the testator and the issue of any deceased members taking by substitution.

(b) Unless the will indicates a contrary intent, if the provisions of subsection (a) of this section do not apply to a devise to a devisee who predeceases the testator, or if a devise otherwise fails, the property shall pass to the residuary devisee or devisees in proportion to their share of the residue. If the devise is a residuary devise, it shall augment the shares of the other residuary devisees, including the shares of any substitute takers under subsection (a) of this section. If there are no residuary devisees, then the property shall pass by intestacy.

(c) Renunciation of a devise is as provided for in Chapter 31B of the General Statutes.

(c1) The determination of whether a devisee has predeceased the testator shall be made as provided by Article 24 of Chapter 28A of the General Statutes.

(d) As used in this section, "devisee" means any person entitled to take real or personal property under the provisions of a will. (1844, c. 88, s. 4; R.C., c. 119, s. 7; Code, s. 2142; Rev., s. 3142; 1919, c. 28; C.S., s. 4166; 1951, c. 762, s. 1; 1953, c. 1084; 1965, c. 938, s. 1; 1975, c. 371, s. 3; 1979, c. 525, s. 5; 1987, c. 86, ss. 1, 2; 1989, c. 244; 1999-145, s. 1; 2001-83, s. 1; 2007-132, ss. 3(a), (b).)

§§ 31-42.1 through 31-42.2. Repealed by Session Laws 1965, c. 938, s. 2.

§ 31-43. When a general gift by will operates as an exercise of power of appointment.

A general devise of the real property of the testator, or of the testator's real property in any place or in the occupation of any person mentioned in the will, or otherwise described in a general manner, shall be construed to include any real property, or any real property to which such description shall extend, as the case may be, which the testator may have power to appoint in any manner the testator may think proper; and shall operate as an exercise of such power, unless a contrary intention shall appear by the will; and in like manner a devise of the personal property of the testator, or any devise of personal property, described in a general manner, shall be construed to include any personal property, or any personal property to which such description shall extend, as the case may be, which the testator may have power to appoint in any manner the testator may think proper, and shall operate as an exercise of such power, unless a contrary intention shall appear by the will. (1844, c. 88, s. 5; R.C., c. 119, s. 8; Code, s. 2143; Rev., s. 3143; C.S., s. 4167; 2011-284, s. 34; 2011-344, s. 8.)

§ 31-44. Repealed by Session Laws 1951, c. 762, s. 2.

§ 31-45: Rewritten and renumbered as G.S. 31-5.5 by Session Laws 1953, c. 1098, s. 7.

§ 31-46. Validity of will; which laws govern.

A will is valid if it meets the requirements of the applicable provisions of law in effect in this State either at the time of its execution or at the time of the death of the testator, or if (i) its execution complies with the law of the place where it is executed at the time of execution; (ii) its execution complies with the law of the place where the testator is domiciled at the time of execution or at the time of death; or (iii) it is a military testamentary instrument executed in accordance with the provisions of 10 U.S.C. § 1044d or any successor or replacement statute. (1953, c. 1098, s. 14; 2013-91, s. 1(g).)

§ 31-46.1. Construction of certain formula clauses applicable to estates of decedents dying in calendar year 2010.

(a) Purpose. - The federal estate tax and generation-skipping transfer tax expired January 1, 2010, for one year. To carry out the intent of decedents in the construction of wills and trusts and to promote judicial economy in the administration of trusts and estates, this section construes certain formula clauses that reference federal estate and generation-skipping transfer tax laws and that are used in wills or codicils of decedents who die in or before calendar year 2010.

(b) Applicability. - This section applies to the following:

(1) To a will or codicil executed by a decedent before December 31, 2009, that contains a formula provision described in subsection (c) of this section if the decedent dies after December 31, 2009, and before the earlier of January 1, 2011, and the effective date of the reinstatement of the federal estate tax and generation-skipping transfer tax, unless the will or codicil clearly manifests an intent that a rule contrary to the rule of construction described in subsection (c) of this section applies.

(2) To the terms of a will or codicil executed by a decedent who dies before December 31, 2009, providing for a disposition of property that contains a formula provision described in subsection (c) of this section and occurs as a result of the death of another individual who dies after December 31, 2009, and before the earlier of January 1, 2011, and the effective date of the reinstatement of the federal estate tax and generation-skipping transfer tax, unless the terms of the will or codicil clearly manifests an intent that a rule contrary to the rule of construction described in subsection (c) of this section applies.

(c) Construction. - A will or codicil subject to this section is considered to refer to the federal estate and generation-skipping transfer tax laws as they applied with respect to estates of decedents dying on December 31, 2009, if the will or codicil contains a formula that meets one or more of the following conditions:

(1) The formula refers to any of the following: "applicable credit amount," "applicable exclusion amount," "applicable exemption amount," "applicable fraction," "estate tax exemption," "generation-skipping transfer tax exemption," "GST exemption," "inclusion ratio," "marital deduction," "maximum marital deduction," "unified credit," or "unlimited marital deduction."

(2) The formula measures a share of an estate or trust based on the amount that can pass free of federal estate taxes or the amount that can pass free of federal generation-skipping transfer taxes.

(3) The formula is otherwise based on a provision of federal estate tax or federal generation-skipping transfer tax law similar to the provisions in subdivision (1) or (2) of this subsection.

(d) Judicial Determination. - The personal representative or an affected beneficiary under a will or testamentary trust may bring an action in the superior court division of the General Court of Justice under Article 26 of Chapter 1 of the

General Statutes, and the trustee of a trust created under the will or an affected beneficiary under the trust may bring a proceeding as permitted under Article 2 of Chapter 36C of the General Statutes to determine whether the decedent intended that the references under subsection (c) of this section be construed with respect to the federal law as it existed after December 31, 2009. The action must be commenced within 12 months following the death of the decedent. (2010-126, s. 1.)

Article 8.

Testamentary Additions to Trusts.

§ 31-47. Testamentary additions to trusts.

(a)   A will may validly devise property to:

(1)   The trustee of a trust established before the testator's death by the testator, by the testator and some other person, or by some other person, including a trust authorized by G.S. 36C-4-401.1; or

(2)   The trustee of a trust to be established at the testator's death, if the trust is identified in the testator's will and its terms are set forth in a written instrument executed before or concurrently with the execution of the testator's will, regardless of the existence, size, or character of the corpus of the trust during the testator's lifetime.

The devise is not invalid because the trust is amendable or revocable, or because the trust instrument or any amendment thereto was not executed in the manner required for wills, or because the trust was amended after the execution of the testator's will or after the testator's death. A revocable trust to which property is first transferred under subdivision (2) of this subsection is an inter vivos trust and not a testamentary trust and, as of the date of the execution of the trust instrument, is subject to Article 6 of Chapter 36C of the General Statutes.

(b)   Unless the testator's will provides otherwise, property devised to the trustee of a trust described in subsection (a) of this section is not held under a testamentary trust of the testator, but it becomes a part of the trust to which it is devised, and shall be administered and disposed of in accordance with the provisions of the governing instrument setting forth the terms of the trust, including any amendments thereto made before or after the testator's death.

(c)   Unless the testator's will provides otherwise, a revocation or termination of the trust before the testator's death causes the devise to lapse.

(d)   A devise to a trust shall be construed as a devise to the trustee of that trust.

(e)   For purposes of this section, "devise," when used as a noun, means a testamentary disposition of real or personal property and, when used as a verb, means to dispose of real or personal property by will.

(f)   Nothing in this section alters, amends, or in any manner affects the application of the doctrine of acts of independent significance. (1955, c. 388; 1957, c. 783, s. 1; 1975, c. 161; 2007-184, s. 1.)

§ 31-48: Reserved for future codification purposes.

§ 31-49: Reserved for future codification purposes.

§ 31-50: Reserved for future codification purposes.

Article 9.

Incorporation by Reference; Acts of Independent Significance.

§ 31-51. Incorporation by reference.

A writing in existence when a will is executed may be incorporated by reference if the language of the will manifests this intent and describes the writing sufficiently to permit its identification. (2007-184, s. 2.)

§ 31-52. Acts and events of independent significance.

A will may dispose of property by reference to acts and events that have significance apart from their effect upon the disposition made by the will, whether they occur before or after the execution of the will or before or after the testator's death. These acts and events may include the execution or revocation of another individual's will and the safekeeping of items in a secured depository. (2007-184, s. 2.)

Chapter 31A.

Acts Barring Property Rights.

Article 1.

Rights of Spouse.

§ 31A-1. Acts barring rights of spouse.

(a) The following persons shall lose the rights specified in subsection (b) of this section:

(1) A spouse from whom or by whom an absolute divorce or marriage annulment has been obtained or from whom a divorce from bed and board has been obtained; or

(2) A spouse who voluntarily separates from the other spouse and lives in adultery and such has not been condoned; or

(3) A spouse who wilfully and without just cause abandons and refuses to live with the other spouse and is not living with the other spouse at the time of such spouse's death; or

(4) A spouse who obtains a divorce the validity of which is not recognized under the laws of this State; or

(5) A spouse who knowingly contracts a bigamous marriage.

(b) The rights lost as specified in subsection (a) of this section shall be as follows:

(1) All rights of intestate succession in the estate of the other spouse;

(2) All right to claim or succeed to a homestead in the real property of the other spouse;

(3) All right to petition for an elective share of the estate of the other spouse and take either the elective intestate share provided or the life interest in lieu thereof;

(4) All right to any year's allowance in the personal property of the other spouse;

(5) All right to administer the estate of the other spouse; and

(6) Any rights or interests in the property of the other spouse which by a settlement before or after marriage were settled upon the offending spouse solely in consideration of the marriage.

(c) Any act specified in subsection (a) of this section may be pleaded in bar of any action or proceeding for the recovery of such rights, interests or estate as set forth in subsection (b) of this section.

(d) The spouse not at fault may sell and convey his or her real and personal property without the joinder of the other spouse, and thereby bar the other spouse of all right, title and interest therein in the following instances:

(1) During the continuance of a separation arising from a divorce from bed and board as specified in subsection (a)(1) of this section, or

(2) During the continuance of a separation arising from adultery as specified in subsection (a)(2) of this section, or during the continuance of a separation arising from an abandonment as specified in subsection (a)(3) of this section, or

(3) When a divorce is granted as specified in subsection (a)(4) of this section, or a bigamous marriage contracted as specified in subsection (a)(5) of this section. (1961, c. 210, s. 1; 1965, c. 850; 2000-178, s. 6.)

Article 2.

Parents.

§ 31A-2. Acts barring rights of parents.

Any parent who has wilfully abandoned the care and maintenance of his or her child shall lose all right to intestate succession in any part of the child's estate and all right to administer the estate of the child, except -

(1) Where the abandoning parent resumed its care and maintenance at least one year prior to the death of the child and continued the same until its death; or

(2) Where a parent has been deprived of the custody of his or her child under an order of a court of competent jurisdiction and the parent has substantially complied with all orders of the court requiring contribution to the support of the child. (1961, c. 210, s. 1.)

Article 3.

Willful and Unlawful Killing of Decedent.

§ 31A-3. Definitions.

As used in this Article, unless the context otherwise requires, the term -

(1) "Decedent" means the person whose life is taken by the slayer as defined in subdivision (3) of this section.

(2) "Property" means any real or personal property and any right or interest therein.

(3) "Slayer" means any of the following:

a. A person who, by a court of competent jurisdiction, is convicted as a principal or accessory before the fact of the willful and unlawful killing of another person.

b. A person who has entered a plea of guilty in open court as a principal or accessory before the fact of the willful and unlawful killing of another person.

c. A person who, upon indictment or information as a principal or accessory before the fact of the willful and unlawful killing of another person, has tendered a plea of nolo contendere which was accepted by the court and judgment entered thereon.

d. A person who is found by a preponderance of the evidence in a civil action brought within two years after the death of the decedent to have willfully and unlawfully killed the decedent or procured the killing of the decedent. If a criminal proceeding is brought against the person to establish the person's guilt as a principal or accessory before the fact of the willful and unlawful killing of the decedent within two years after the death of the decedent, the civil action may be brought within 90 days after a final determination is made by a court of competent jurisdiction in that criminal proceeding or within the original two years after the death of the decedent, whichever is later. The burden of proof in the civil action is on the party seeking to establish that the killing was willful and unlawful for the purposes of this Article.

e. A juvenile who is adjudicated delinquent by reason of committing an act that, if committed by an adult, would make the adult a principal or accessory before the fact of the willful and unlawful killing of another person.

The term "slayer" does not include a person who is found not guilty by reason of insanity of being a principal or accessory before the fact of the willful and unlawful killing of another person. (1961, c. 210, s. 1; 2006-107, s. 1.)

§ 31A-4. Slayer barred from testate or intestate succession and other rights.

The slayer shall be deemed to have died immediately prior to the death of the decedent and the following rules shall apply:

(1) The slayer shall not acquire any property or receive any benefit from the estate of the decedent by testate or intestate succession or by common law or statutory right as surviving spouse of the decedent.

(2) Where the decedent dies intestate as to property which would have passed to the slayer by intestate succession and the slayer has living issue who would have been entitled to an interest in the property if the slayer had predeceased the decedent, the property shall be distributed to such issue, per stirpes. If the slayer does not have such issue, then the property shall be distributed as though the slayer had predeceased the decedent.

(3) Where the decedent dies testate as to property which would have passed to the slayer pursuant to the will, the devolution of such property shall be governed by G.S. 31-42(a) notwithstanding the fact the slayer has not actually died before the decedent. (1961, c. 210, s. 1; 1999-296, s. 1.)

§ 31A-5. Entirety property.

Where the slayer and decedent hold property as tenants by the entirety, one half of the property shall pass upon the death of the decedent to the decedent's estate, and the other one half shall be held by the slayer during his or her life, subject to pass upon the slayer's death to the slain decedent's heirs or devisees as defined in G.S. 28A-1-1. (1961, c. 210, s. 1; 1979, c. 572.)

§ 31A-6. Survivorship property.

(a) Where the slayer and the decedent hold property with right of survivorship as joint tenants, joint owners, joint obligees or otherwise, the decedent's share thereof shall pass immediately upon the death of the decedent to his estate, and the slayer's share shall be held by the slayer during his lifetime and at his death shall pass to the estate of the decedent. During his lifetime, the slayer shall have the right to the income from his share of the property subject to the rights of creditors of the slayer.

(b) Where three or more persons, including the slayer and the decedent, hold property with right of survivorship as joint tenants, joint owners, joint obligees or otherwise, the portion of the decedent's share which would have accrued to the slayer as a result of the death of the decedent shall pass to the estate of the decedent. If the slayer becomes the final survivor, one half of the property then held by the slayer shall pass immediately to the estate of the decedent, and upon the death of the slayer the remaining interest of the slayer shall pass to the estate of the decedent. During his lifetime the slayer shall have the right to the income from his share of the property subject to the rights of creditors of the slayer. (1961, c. 210, s. 1.)

§ 31A-7. Reversions and vested remainders.

(a) Where the slayer holds a reversion or vested remainder in property subject to a life estate in the decedent and the slayer would have obtained the right of present possession upon the death of the decedent, such property shall pass to the estate of the decedent during the period of the life expectancy of the decedent.

(b) Where the slayer holds a reversion or vested remainder in property subject to a life estate in a third person which is measured by the life of the decedent, such property shall remain in the possession of the third person during the period of the life expectancy of the decedent. (1961, c. 210, s. 1.)

§ 31A-8. Contingent remainders and executory interests.

As to any contingent remainder or executory or other future interest held by the slayer subject to become vested in him or increased in any way for him upon the condition of the death of the decedent:

(1) If the interest would not have become vested or increased if he had predeceased the decedent, he shall be deemed to have so predeceased the decedent; but

(2) In any case, the interest shall not be vested or increased during the period of the life expectancy of the decedent. (1961, c. 210, s. 1.)

§ 31A-9. Divesting of interests in property.

Where the slayer holds any interest in property, whether vested or not, subject to be divested, diminished in any way or extinguished if the decedent survives him or lives to a certain age, such interest shall be held by the slayer during his lifetime or until the decedent would have reached such age but shall then pass as if the decedent had died immediately after the death of the slayer or the reaching of such age. (1961, c. 210, s. 1.)

§ 31A-10. Powers of appointment and revocation.

(a) As to any exercise in the will of the decedent of a power of appointment in favor of the slayer, the slayer shall be deemed to have predeceased the decedent and the slayer shall not acquire any property or receive any benefit by virtue of such appointment and the appointed property shall pass in accordance with the applicable lapse statute, if any.

(b) Property held either presently or in remainder by the slayer subject to be divested by the exercise by the decedent of a power of revocation or a general power of appointment shall pass to the estate of the decedent; and property so held by the slayer subject to be divested by the exercise by the decedent of a power of appointment to a particular person or persons or to a class of persons shall pass to such person or persons or in equal shares to the members of such class of persons, exclusive of the slayer. (1961, c. 210, s. 1.)

§ 31A-11. Insurance benefits.

(a) Insurance and annuity proceeds payable to the slayer:

(1) As the beneficiary or assignee of any policy or certificate of insurance on the life of the decedent, or

(2) In any other manner payable to the slayer by virtue of his surviving the decedent, shall be paid to the person or persons who would have been entitled thereto as if the slayer had predeceased the decedent. If no alternate beneficiary is named, insurance and annuity proceeds shall be paid into the estate of the decedent.

(b) If the decedent is beneficiary or assignee of any policy or certificate of insurance on the life of the slayer, the proceeds shall be paid to the estate of the decedent upon the death of the slayer, unless the policy names some person other than the slayer or his estate as alternative beneficiary.

(c) Any insurance or annuity company making payment according to the terms of its policy or contract shall not be subjected to additional liability by the terms of this chapter if such payment or performance is made without notice of circumstances tending to bring it within the provisions of this Chapter. (1961, c. 210, s. 1; 1989, c. 485, s. 3.)

§ 31A-12. Persons acquiring from slayer protected.

The provisions of this Chapter shall not affect the right of any person who, before the interests of the slayer have been adjudicated, acquires from the slayer for adequate consideration property or an interest therein which the slayer would have received except for the terms of this Chapter, provided the same is acquired without notice of circumstances tending to bring it within the provisions of this Chapter; but all consideration received by the slayer shall be held by him in trust for the persons entitled to the property under the provisions of this Chapter, and the slayer shall also be liable both for any portion of such consideration which he may have dissipated, and for any difference between the actual value of the property and the amount of such consideration. (1961, c. 210, s. 1.)

§ 31A-12.1. Remedies to be exclusive.

This Article wholly supplants the common law rule preventing a person whose culpable negligence causes the death of a decedent from succeeding to any property passing by reason of the death of the decedent. (2006-107, s. 2.)

Article 4.

General Provisions.

§ 31A-13. Record determining slayer admissible in evidence.

The record of the judicial proceeding in which the slayer was determined to be such, pursuant to G.S. 31A-3 of this Chapter, shall be admissible in evidence for or against a claimant of property in any civil action arising under this Chapter. (1961, c. 210, s. 1.)

§ 31A-14. Revised Simultaneous Death Act not applicable.

The Revised Simultaneous Death Act, Article 24 of Chapter 28A of the General Statutes, shall not apply to cases governed by this Chapter. (1961, c. 210, s. 1; 1979, c. 107, s. 5; 2007-132, s. 4.)

§ 31A-15. Chapter to be broadly construed.

This Chapter shall not be considered penal in nature, but shall be construed broadly in order to effect the policy of this State that no person shall be allowed to profit by his own wrong. As to all acts specifically provided for in this Chapter, the rules, remedies, and procedures herein specified shall be exclusive, and as to all acts not specifically provided for in this Chapter, all rules, remedies, and procedures, if any, which now exist or hereafter may exist either by virtue of statute, or by virtue of the inherent powers of any court of competent jurisdiction, or otherwise, shall be applicable. (1961, c. 210, s. 1.)

Chapter 31B.

Renunciation of Property and Renunciation of Fiduciary Powers Act.

§ 31B-1. Right to renounce succession.

(a) A person who succeeds to a property interest as:

(1) Heir;

(2) Next of kin;

(3) Devisee;

(4) Repealed by Session Laws 2011-284, s. 35, effective June 24, 2011.

(4a) Donee;

(5) Beneficiary of a life insurance policy who did not possess the incidents of ownership under the policy at the time of death of the insured;

(6) Person succeeding to a renounced interest;

(7) Beneficiary under a testamentary trust or under an inter vivos trust;

(8) Appointee under a power of appointment exercised by a testamentary instrument or a nontestamentary instrument;

(9) Repealed by Session Laws 1989, c. 684, s. 2.

(9a) Surviving joint tenant, surviving tenant by the entireties, or surviving tenant of a tenancy with a right of survivorship;

(9b) Person entitled to share in a testator's estate under the provisions of G.S. 31-5.5;

(9c) Beneficiary under any other testamentary or nontestamentary instrument, including a beneficiary under:

a. Any qualified or nonqualified deferred compensation, employee benefit, retirement or death benefit, plan, fund, annuity, contract, policy, program or instrument, either funded or unfunded, which is established or maintained to provide retirement income or death benefits or results in, or is intended to result in, deferral of income;

b. An individual retirement account or individual retirement annuity; or

c. Any annuity, payable on death account, or other right to death benefits arising under contract;

(9d) Duly authorized or appointed guardian of any of the persons listed in subdivisions (1) through (9c) of this subsection, but only with the prior or subsequent approval of the clerk of superior court, or if required, of the resident judge of the superior court, pursuant to a proceeding or action instituted in accordance with and subject to the requirements of G.S. 31B-1.2; or

(9e) Subject to G.S. 31B-1.1 and G.S. 31B-1.2, fiduciary, including a trustee of a charitable trust, an attorney-in-fact of any of the persons listed in subdivisions (1) through (9e) of this subsection if expressly authorized by the governing power of attorney, and a personal representative appointed under Chapter 28A of the General Statutes of any of the persons listed in subdivisions (1) through (9c) of this subsection;

(10) Repealed by Session Laws 2009-48, s. 1, effective October 1, 2009.

may renounce at anytime, in whole or in part, the right of succession to any property or interest therein, including a future interest, by filing a written instrument under the provisions of this Chapter. A renunciation may be of a fractional share or any limited interest or estate. The renunciation shall be deemed to include the entire interest of the person whose property or interest is being renounced unless otherwise specifically limited. A person may renounce any interest in or power over property, including a power of appointment, even if its creator imposed a spendthrift provision or similar restriction on transfer or a restriction or limitation on the right to renounce. Notwithstanding the foregoing, there shall be no right of partial renunciation if the instrument creating the interest expressly so provides.

(b) This Chapter shall apply to all renunciations of present and future interests, whether qualified or nonqualified for federal and State inheritance, estate, and gift tax purposes, unless expressly provided otherwise in the instrument creating the interest.

(c) The instrument of renunciation shall (i) identify the transferor of the property or interest in the property or the creator of the power or the holder of the power, (ii) describe the property or interest renounced, (iii) declare the renunciation and extent thereof, and (iv) be signed and acknowledged by the person renouncing.

(d) A parent of a minor for whom no general guardian or guardian of the estate has been appointed may renounce, in whole or in part, an interest in or power over property (including a power of appointment) that would have passed to the minor as the result of that parent's renunciation. The parent may renounce the interest or power even if its creator imposed a spendthrift provision or similar restriction on transfer or a restriction or limitation on the right to renounce. (1975, c. 371, s. 1; 1983, c. 66, s. 1; 1989, c. 684, s. 2; 1998-148, s. 1; 2009-48, s. 1; 2011-284, s. 35.)

§ 31B-1.1. Right of fiduciary to renounce.

(a)   Except as otherwise provided in the testamentary or nontestamentary instrument, a fiduciary under a testamentary or nontestamentary instrument may renounce, in whole or in part, fiduciary rights, privileges, powers, and immunities; however, a fiduciary may not renounce the personal rights exercisable by a beneficiary alone, unless the instrument creating the fiduciary relationship authorizes such a renunciation. The instrument of renunciation shall (i) identify the creator of the rights, powers, privileges, or immunities, (ii) describe any right, power, privilege, or immunity renounced, (iii) declare the renunciation and the extent thereof, and (iv) be signed and acknowledged by the fiduciary authorized to renounce.

(b)   Except as provided in subsection (c) of this section and except to the extent a statute of this State expressly restricts or limits a fiduciary's right to renounce, a fiduciary acting in a fiduciary capacity may renounce the right of succession to any property or interest therein as permitted by this Chapter, even if the testamentary or nontestamentary instrument governing the fiduciary restricts or limits the right to renounce the fiduciary's right of succession to the property or interest therein.

(c)   An attorney-in-fact for a principal acting under subsection (a) or subsection (b) of this section may renounce only if expressly authorized by the governing power of attorney. (1989, c. 684, s. 3; 2009-48, s. 2.)

§ 31B-1.2. Right of fiduciary to institute a proceeding for review of renunciation.

(a)   Prior to renouncing, if a fiduciary so elects, the fiduciary may institute a proceeding by petition before the clerk of court for a determination as to whether a renunciation would be compatible with the fiduciary's duties. In the case of a trustee, commencement of the proceeding, jurisdiction, venue, parties, representation, and notice shall be governed by Chapter 36C of the General Statutes. In the case of a personal representative, commencement of the proceeding, jurisdiction, venue, parties, representation, and notice shall be governed by Chapter 28A of the General Statutes. In addition to any other notice requirements, notice of the proceeding shall be given to all persons entitled to delivery of a copy of an instrument of renunciation under G.S. 31B-2.1.

(b) After renouncing, if a fiduciary so elects, the fiduciary has a right to institute a declaratory judgment action pursuant to Article 26 of Chapter 1 of the General Statutes for a determination as to whether the renunciation is compatible with the fiduciary's duties. In addition to any other notice requirements, notice of the action shall be given to all persons entitled to delivery of a copy of an instrument of renunciation under G.S. 31B-2.1.

(c) A proceeding or action instituted under this section shall comply with all of the following:

(1) The petition or complaint shall state the basis for the fiduciary's allegation that the renunciation is compatible with the fiduciary's duties, considering among other things the intended purposes of the trust or other instrument and the impact of the renunciation on beneficiaries and potential beneficiaries. A petition or complaint filed by a trustee of a charitable trust shall contain a statement that a copy of the petition or complaint is being provided to the Attorney General.

(2) After considering among other things the intended purposes of the trust or other instrument and the impact of the renunciation on beneficiaries and potential beneficiaries, the court shall enter an order stating the court's determination as to whether the renunciation is compatible with the fiduciary's duties.

(d) The effectiveness of a renunciation is not affected by a determination under this section that the renunciation is not compatible with a fiduciary's duties. (2009-48, s. 3; 2011-344, s. 9.)

§ 31B-1A: Recodified as G.S. 31B-1.1.

§ 31B-2. Filing and registering of renunciations; failure to file or register; spouse's interest.

(a) To be a qualified disclaimer for federal and State inheritance, estate, and gift tax purposes, an instrument of renunciation shall be filed within the time period required under the applicable federal statute for a renunciation to be given effect as a disclaimer for federal estate and gift tax purposes. If there is no such federal statute the instrument shall be filed not later than nine months after the date the transfer of the renounced interest to the person whose property or interest is being renounced was complete for the purpose of such taxes.

(b) When a renunciation of real property or an interest in real property is made within the time period required under subsection (a) of this section, the spouse of the person whose property or interest is being renounced is not required to join in the execution of the instrument of renunciation, and, as provided in G.S. 31B-3(a)(1), the spouse has no statutory dower, inchoate marital rights, elective share, or any other marital interest in the real property or real property interest renounced.

(c) The renunciation is effective when filed with the clerk of court (i) in the county in which court proceedings have been commenced for the administration of the estate of the deceased owner or deceased creator of the power or holder of the power; or (ii) if proceedings have not been commenced, then in a county in which they could be commenced; or (iii) in all other cases, in a county with a court that has jurisdiction to enforce the terms of the instrument creating the interest renounced. In those cases in which an estate proceeding has not been commenced, the renunciation shall be filed as an estate matter. In addition to the above requirements, a renunciation of real property, or an interest therein, shall be registered in accordance with the provisions of subsection (d) of this section.

(d) If real property or an interest therein is renounced, the instrument of renunciation shall also be registered as provided in G.S. 47-18 or G.S. 47-20. The instrument of renunciation shall be indexed in the grantor's index under (i) the name of the transferor or creator of the power or holder of the power, and (ii) the name of the person whose property or interest is being renounced. Failure to file or register the instrument of renunciation does not affect the effectiveness of the renunciation as between the person whose property or interest is being renounced and persons to whom the property interest or power passes by reason of the renunciation; however, record title to a renounced interest in real property does not pass to persons receiving the renounced interest by reason of the renunciation until the instrument of renunciation is registered as provided in G.S. 47-18 or G.S. 47-20.

(e) If an instrument transferring an interest in or right, privilege, power, or immunity over property subject to a renunciation is required or permitted by law to be filed or registered, the instrument of renunciation may be so filed or registered. Failure to file or register the instrument of renunciation does not affect the effectiveness of the renunciation as between the person whose property or interest is being renounced and persons to whom the property interest or power passes by reason of the renunciation. (1975, c. 371, s. 1; 1979, c. 525, s. 7; 1983, c. 66, s. 2; 1989, c. 684, s. 4; 1991, c. 744, s. 1; 1998-148, s. 2; 2009-48, s. 4.)

§ 31B-2.1. Delivery to other persons of instrument of renunciation by the person renouncing.

(a) In this section:

(1) "Beneficiary designation" means an instrument, other than an instrument creating a trust, naming the beneficiary of:

a. An annuity or insurance policy;

b. An account with a designation for payment on death;

c. A security registered in beneficiary form;

d. A pension, profitsharing, retirement, or other employment-related benefit plan;

e. An individual retirement account or retirement annuity; or

f. Any other nonprobate transfer at death.

(2) "Deliver" means to deliver in person or to send, properly addressed, by first-class mail, telephonic facsimile transmission equipment, electronic mail, or third-party commercial carrier, or by any method permitted by G.S. 1A-1, Rule 4.

(b) The failure to deliver a copy of an instrument of renunciation by a method permitted by G.S. 1A-1, Rule 4, or by a method that results in actual receipt tolls any statute of limitations with regard to any right of action for breach of fiduciary duty.

(c) If a fiduciary renounces an interest in property pursuant to G.S. 31B-1(a)(9e), a copy of the instrument of renunciation shall be delivered to each living person whose beneficial interest is affected by the renunciation and to any co-fiduciary who did not join in the renunciation.

(d) In the case of an interest created under the law of intestate succession or an interest created by will, other than an interest in a testamentary trust, a copy of the instrument of renunciation must:

(1) Be delivered to the personal representative of the decedent's estate; or

(2) If no personal representative is then serving, be filed as an estate matter with a court having jurisdiction to appoint the personal representative.

(e) In the case of a beneficiary renouncing an interest in a testamentary trust, a copy of the instrument of renunciation must:

(1) Be delivered to the trustee then serving;

(2) If no trustee is then serving, be delivered to the personal representative of the decedent's estate; or

(3) If no personal representative or trustee is then serving, be filed as an estate matter with a court having jurisdiction to enforce the trust.

(f) In the case of a beneficiary renouncing an interest in an inter vivos trust, a copy of the instrument of renunciation must:

(1) Be delivered to the trustee then serving;

(2) Except as provided in subdivision (3) of this subsection, if no trustee is then serving, be filed as an estate matter with a court having jurisdiction to enforce the trust; or

(3) If the renunciation is made before the time the instrument creating the trust becomes irrevocable, be delivered to the settlor of the trust or the transferor of the interest.

(g) In the case of a beneficiary renouncing an interest created by a beneficiary designation made before the time the designation becomes irrevocable, a copy of the instrument of renunciation must be delivered to the person making the beneficiary designation.

(h) In the case of a beneficiary renouncing an interest created by a beneficiary designation made after the time the designation becomes irrevocable, a copy of the instrument of renunciation must be delivered to the person obligated to distribute the interest.

(i) In the case of a renunciation by a surviving holder of an interest in property subject to a right of survivorship, a copy of the instrument of renunciation must be delivered to the persons to whom the person renouncing reasonably believes the renounced interest passes, at their last addresses known to the person renouncing, and to the personal representative of the deceased joint holder, if any.

(j) In the case of a renunciation by a permissible appointee, or taker in default of exercise, of a power of appointment at anytime after the power was created, a copy of the instrument of renunciation must be delivered:

(1) To the holder of the power;

(2) To the fiduciary acting under the instrument that created the power or, if no fiduciary is then serving under the instrument that created the power, filed as an estate matter with a court having authority to appoint the fiduciary; and

(3) To any holder of legal title to the property subject to the power of appointment other than the fiduciary.

(k) In the case of a renunciation by an appointee of an exercised power of appointment, a copy of the instrument of renunciation must be delivered:

(1) To the holder of the power or the personal representative of the holder's estate;

(2) To the fiduciary under the instrument that created the power or, if no fiduciary is then serving under the instrument that created the power, filed as an estate matter with a court having authority to appoint the fiduciary; and

(3) To any holder of legal title to the property subject to the power of appointment other than the fiduciary.

(l) In the case of a renunciation of a power of appointment by the holder of the power, a copy of the instrument of renunciation must be delivered:

(1) To the fiduciary acting under the instrument that created the power or, if no fiduciary is then serving under the instrument that created the power, filed as an estate matter with a court having authority to appoint the fiduciary; and

(2) To any holder of legal title to the property subject to the power of appointment other than the fiduciary.

(m) In the case of a renunciation by a fiduciary of a right, privilege, power, or immunity relating to a trust or estate, a copy of the instrument of renunciation must be delivered as provided in subsection (c), (d), (e), or (f) of this section, as if the power renounced were an interest in property.

(n) In the case of a renunciation of a power by an agent, including an attorney-in-fact, a copy of the instrument of renunciation must be delivered to the principal or the principal's legal representative other than the agent.

(o) In the case of a renunciation by a trustee of a charitable trust, a copy of the instrument of renunciation must be delivered to the North Carolina Attorney General in addition to any other delivery required by this section.

(p) In the case of a renunciation by a donee, a copy of the instrument of renunciation must be delivered to the persons to whom the person renouncing reasonably believes the renounced interest passes, at their last addresses known to the person renouncing, and to the donor or the donor's legal representative other than the donee.

(q) The failure to deliver a copy of the instrument of renunciation as required in this section does not affect the validity of the renunciation for purposes of G.S. 31B-3 even though the renunciation may not be recognized as a disclaimer for federal estate tax purposes. (2009-48, s. 5.)

§ 31B-3. Effect of renunciation.

(a) Unless the decedent, donee of a power of appointment, or creator of an interest under an inter vivos instrument has otherwise provided in the instrument creating the interest, the property or interest renounced devolves as follows:

(1) If the renunciation is filed within the time period described in G.S. 31B-2(a), the property or interest renounced devolves and any interest that takes effect in possession or enjoyment after the termination of the property or interest renounced takes effect as if the person whose property or interest is being renounced had predeceased the date the transfer of the renounced interest was complete for federal and State inheritance, estate, and gift tax purposes, or, in the case of the renunciation of a fiduciary right, power, privilege, or immunity, the property or interest subject to the power devolves as if the fiduciary right, power, privilege, or immunity never existed. Any such renunciation relates back for all purposes to the date the transfer of the renounced interest was complete for the purpose of those taxes, and the spouse of the person whose property or interest is being renounced has no elective share or other marital interest in the renounced property.

(2) If the renunciation is not filed within the time period described in G.S. 31B-2(a), the person whose property or interest is being renounced is deemed to have made a transfer of the property or interest and the property or interest devolves and any interest that takes effect in possession or enjoyment after the termination of the property or interest renounced takes effect as if the person whose property or interest is being renounced had died on the date the renunciation is filed, or, in the case of the renunciation of a fiduciary right, power, privilege, or immunity, the property or interest subject to the power devolves as if the fiduciary right, power, privilege, or immunity ceased to exist as of the date the renunciation is filed.

(3) Any future interest that takes effect in possession or enjoyment after the termination of the estate or interest renounced takes effect as if the person whose property or interest is being renounced had died on the date determined under subdivision (1) or (2) of this subsection, and upon the filing of the renunciation the persons in being as of the time the person whose property or interest is being renounced is deemed to have died will immediately become entitled to possession or enjoyment of any such future interest.

(b) In the event that the property or interest renounced was created by testamentary disposition, the devolution of the property or interest renounced shall be as provided in G.S. 31-42 notwithstanding that in fact the person whose property or interest is being renounced has not actually died before the testator.

(c) In the event that the decedent dies intestate, or the ownership or succession to property or to an interest is to be determined as though a decedent had died intestate, and the person whose property or interest is being renounced has living issue who would have been entitled to an interest in the property or interest if the person whose property or interest is being renounced had predeceased the decedent, then the property or interest renounced shall be distributed to such issue, per stirpes. If the person whose property or interest is being renounced does not have such issue, then the property or interest shall be distributed as though the person whose property or interest is being renounced had predeceased the decedent.

(d) In the event that the property or interest renounced was created by a revocable or irrevocable inter vivos trust, the devolution of the property or interest renounced shall be as provided in G.S. 36C-6-605 notwithstanding that in fact the person whose property or interest is being renounced has not actually died before the event that would otherwise cause the property or interest renounced to pass to the person whose property or interest is being renounced.

(e) If a trustee files, within the time period described in G.S. 31B-2(a), a renunciation of an interest in property, the interest does not become trust property. If a trustee does not file a renunciation of an interest in property within the time period described in G.S. 31B-2(a), the interest passes to the person or persons who would have taken the interest as of the date of the renunciation if the trust had never existed.

(f) Except as provided in the instrument of renunciation, if a renunciation causes property to pass to a trust in which the person whose property or interest is being renounced holds a power of appointment, the person renouncing is deemed to have renounced the power of appointment with respect to assets passing into the trust by reason of the renunciation if the person renouncing is a person who holds a right to renounce the power of appointment.

(g) Unless otherwise provided in the instrument of renunciation, the interest in property being renounced by a surviving tenant by the entireties upon the death of the other tenant is deemed to be a one-half interest in the former entirety property, and title to that one-half interest passes as if the deceased tenant survived the tenant renouncing.

(h) Unless otherwise provided in the instrument of renunciation, the interest in property being renounced by a surviving joint tenant with right of survivorship is deemed to be the fractional interest of the deceased joint tenant to which the surviving joint tenant would have been entitled by right of survivorship, and title to that fractional interest passes as if the tenant renouncing predeceased the deceased joint tenant.

(i),(j) Reserved for future codification purposes.

(k) A renunciation is binding upon the person whose property or interest is being renounced and all persons claiming through or under that person. (1975, c. 371, s. 1; 1979, c. 525, s. 6; 1989, c. 684, s. 5; 1993, c. 308, ss. 1, 2; 1998-148, s. 3; 2009-48, s. 6.)

§ 31B-4. Waiver and bar.

(a) The right to renounce property or an interest therein is barred by:

(1) An assignment, conveyance, encumbrance, pledge, or transfer of the property or interest, or a contract therefor by the person authorized to renounce,

(2) A written waiver of the right to renounce, or

(3) Repealed by Session Laws 1998-148, s. 4.

(4) A sale of the property or interest under judicial sale made before the renunciation is effected.

(b) An instrument waiving or barring the right to renounce is binding upon the person waiving the right to renounce or the person barred from renouncing and all persons claiming through or under that person.

(c) A fiduciary's application for appointment or assumption of duties as fiduciary does not waive or bar the fiduciary's right to renounce a right, power, privilege, or immunity.

(d) No person shall be liable for distributing or disposing of property in reliance upon the terms of a renunciation that is invalid for the reason that the right of renunciation has been waived or barred, if the distribution or disposition is otherwise proper, and the person has no actual knowledge or record notice of the facts that constitute a waiver or bar to the right of renunciation.

(e) The right to renounce property or an interest in property pursuant to this Chapter is not barred by an acceptance of the property, interest, or benefit thereunder; provided, however, an acceptance of the property, interest, or benefit thereunder may preclude such renunciation from being a qualified renunciation for federal and State inheritance, estate, and gift tax purposes.

(f) An instrument waiving or barring the right to renounce an interest in real property is not effective as to persons protected under G.S. 47-18 or G.S. 47-20 until either (i) registered as provided in those sections or (ii) registered pursuant to a judicial sale proceeding as described in subdivision (4) of subsection (a) of this section in which the person renouncing is a party. The instrument of waiver or bar shall be indexed in the grantor's index under (i) the name of the transferor of the property or interest in the property or creator of the power or holder of the power and (ii) the name of the person whose renunciation is waived or barred. (1975, c. 371, s. 1; 1989, c. 684, s. 6; 1998-148, ss. 4, 5; 2000-140, s. 8; 2009-48, s. 7.)

§ 31B-4.1. Tax qualified renunciation.

If, as a result of a renunciation, the renounced property is treated pursuant to the provisions of Title 26 of the United States Code, as now or hereafter amended, or any successor statute thereto, and the regulations promulgated thereunder, as never having been transferred to the person whose property or interest is being renounced, then the renunciation is an effective renunciation, notwithstanding any other provision of this Chapter. This section does not preclude an action for breach of fiduciary duty. (2009-48, s. 8.)

§ 31B-5. Exclusiveness of remedy.

This Chapter does not exclude or abridge any other rights or procedures existing under any other statute or otherwise provided by law to waive, release, refuse to accept, disclaim or renounce property or an interest therein, or any fiduciary right, power, privilege, or immunity. (1975, c. 371, s. 1; 1989, c. 684, s. 7.)

§ 31B-6: Repealed by Session Laws 2009-48, s. 9, effective October 1, 2009, and applicable to renunciations and powers of attorney executed on or after that date.

§ 31B-7. Short title.

This Chapter may be cited as the Renunciation of Property and Renunciation of Fiduciary Powers Act. (1975, c. 371, s. 1; 1989 (Reg. Sess., 1990), c. 1024, s. 11.)

Chapter 31C.

Uniform Disposition of Community Property Rights at Death Act.

§ 31C-1. Application.

This Chapter applies to the disposition at death of the following property acquired by a married person:

(1)   All personal property, wherever situated:

a.   Which was acquired as or became, and remained, community property under the laws of another jurisdiction; or

b.   All or the proportionate part of that property acquired with the rents, issues, or income of, or the proceeds from, or in exchange for, that community property; or

c.   Traceable to that community property;

(2)   All or the proportionate part of any real property situated in this State which was acquired with the rents, issues or income of, the proceeds from, or in exchange for, property acquired as or which became, and remained, community property under the laws of another jurisdiction, or property traceable to that community property. (1981, c. 882, s. 1.)

§ 31C-2. Rebuttable presumptions.

In determining whether this Chapter applies to specific property the following rebuttable presumptions apply:

(1)   Property acquired during marriage by a spouse of that marriage while domiciled in a jurisdiction under whose laws property could then be acquired as community property is presumed to have been acquired as or to have become, and remained, property to which this Chapter applies; and

(2)   Real property situated in this State and personal property wherever situated, acquired by a married person while domiciled in a jurisdiction under whose laws property could not then be acquired as community property, title to which was taken in a form which created rights of survivorship, is presumed not to be property to which this Chapter applies. (1981, c. 882, s. 1.)

§ 31C-3. Disposition of community property upon death.

Upon death of a married person, one half of the property to which this Chapter applies is the property of the surviving spouse and is not subject to testamentary disposition by the decedent or distribution under the laws of succession of this State. One half of that property is the property of the decedent and is subject to testamentary disposition or distribution under the laws of succession of this State. With respect to property to which this Chapter applies, the one half of the property of the decedent is not subject to the surviving spouse's right to petition for an elective share under the provisions of Article 1A of Chapter 30, and is not subject to the right to elect a life estate under the provisions of Article 8 of Chapter 29. (1981, c. 882, s. 1; 2000-178, s. 7.)

§ 31C-4. Perfection of title of surviving spouse.

If the title to any property to which this Chapter applies was held by the decedent at the time of death, or by a trustee of a revocable inter vivos trust created by the decedent, title of the surviving spouse may be perfected by an order of the clerk of superior court who appointed the decedent's personal representative or by execution of an instrument by the personal representative or the heirs or devisees of the decedent with the approval of the said clerk.

Neither the personal representative nor the court in which the decedent's estate is being administered has a duty to discover or attempt to discover whether property held by the decedent is property to which this Chapter applies, unless a written demand is made by the surviving spouse or the spouse's successor in interest. (1981, c. 882, s. 1.)

§ 31C-5. Perfection of title of personal representative, heir or devisee; duty of personal representative.

If the title to any property to which this Chapter applies is held by the surviving spouse at the time of the decedent's death, the personal representative or an heir or devisee of the decedent may institute an action to perfect title to the property. The personal representative has no fiduciary duty to discover or attempt to discover whether any property held by the surviving spouse is property to which this Chapter applies, unless a written demand is made by an heir, devisee, or creditor of the decedent. (1981, c. 882, s. 1.)

§ 31C-6. Written demand.

(a) Written demand in this Chapter shall be made by a surviving spouse, the spouse's successor in interest, or the decedent's heirs or devisees not later than six months after the decedent's will has been admitted to probate, or not later than six months after the appointment of an administrator if there is no will, or not later than six months after the decedent's death if the property to which this Chapter applies is held in an inter vivos trust created by the decedent; and written demand by a creditor of the decedent shall be made within the period for presentation of a claim against the decedent's estate as set out in Article 19 of Chapter 28A.

(b) Written demand in this Chapter shall be delivered in person or by registered mail to the personal representative. As used in this Chapter, the personal representative may also mean the trustee of an inter vivos trust created by the decedent who has legal title to, or possession of, the property to which this Chapter applies. (1981, c. 882, s. 1.)

§ 31C-7. Purchaser for value or lender.

(a)   If a surviving spouse has apparent title to property to which this Chapter applies, a purchaser for value or a lender taking a security interest in the property takes his interest in the property free of any rights of the personal representative or an heir or devisee of the decedent.

(b)   If a personal representative or an heir or devisee of the decedent has apparent title to property to which this Chapter applies, a purchaser for value or a lender taking a security interest in the property takes his interest in the property free of any rights of the surviving spouse.

(c)   A purchaser for value or a lender need not inquire whether a vendor or borrower acted properly.

(d)   The proceeds of a sale or creation of a security interest shall be treated in the same manner as the property transferred to the purchaser for value or a lender. (1981, c. 882, s. 1.)

§ 31C-8. Creditors' rights.

This Chapter does not affect rights of creditors with respect to property to which this Chapter applies. (1981, c. 882, s. 1.)

§ 31C-9. Severing or altering of married persons.

This Chapter does not prevent married persons from severing or altering their interests in property to which this Chapter applies. (1981, c. 882, s. 1.)

§ 31C-10. Limitations on testamentary disposition.

This Chapter does not authorize a person to dispose of property by will if it is held under limitations imposed by law preventing testamentary disposition by that person. (1981, c. 882, s. 1.)

§ 31C-11. Uniformity of application and construction.

This Chapter shall be so applied and construed as to effectuate its general purpose to make uniform the law with respect to the subject of this Chapter among those states which enact it. (1981, c. 882, s. 1.)

§ 31C-12. Short title.

Chapter 32.

Fiduciaries.

Article 1.

Uniform Fiduciaries Act.

§ 32-1. Short title.

This Article may be cited as the Uniform Fiduciaries Act. (1923, c. 85, s. 14; C.S., s. 1864(d); 1965, c. 628, s. 2.)

§ 32-2. Definition of terms.

(a)   In this Article unless the context or subject matter otherwise requires:

"Bank" includes any person or association of persons, whether incorporated or not, carrying on the business of banking.

"Fiduciary" includes a trustee under any trust, expressed, implied, resulting or constructive, executor, administrator, guardian, conservator, curator, receiver, trustee in bankruptcy, assignee for the benefit of creditors, partner, agent, officer of a corporation, public or private, public officer, or any other person acting in a fiduciary capacity for any person, trust or estate.

"Person" includes a corporation, partnership, or other association, or two or more persons having a joint or common interest.

"Principal" includes any person to whom a fiduciary as such owes an obligation.

(b) A thing is done "in good faith" within the meaning of this Article when it is in fact done honestly, whether it be done negligently or not. (1923, c. 85, s. 1; C.S., s. 1864(e); 1965, c. 628, s. 2.)

§ 32-3. Application of payments made to fiduciaries.

A person who in good faith pays or transfers to a fiduciary any money or other property, which the fiduciary as such is authorized to receive, is not responsible for the proper application thereof by the fiduciary; and any right or title acquired from the fiduciary in consideration of such payment or transfer is not invalid in consequence of a misapplication by the fiduciary. (1923, c. 85, s. 2; C.S., s. 1864(f).)

§ 32-4. Repealed by Session Laws 1977, c. 814, s. 8, effective January 1, 1978.

§ 32-5. Transfer of negotiable instrument by fiduciary.

If any negotiable instrument payable or indorsed to a fiduciary as such is indorsed by a fiduciary, or if any negotiable instrument payable or indorsed to his principal is indorsed by a fiduciary empowered to indorse such instrument on behalf of his principal, the indorsee is not bound to inquire whether the fiduciary is committing a breach of his obligation as fiduciary in indorsing or delivering the instrument, and is not chargeable with notice that the fiduciary is committing a breach of his obligation as fiduciary unless he takes the instrument with actual knowledge of such breach or with knowledge of such facts that his action in taking the instrument amounts to bad faith. If, however, such instrument is transferred by the fiduciary in payment of or as security for a personal debt of the fiduciary to the actual knowledge of the creditor, or is transferred in any transaction known by the transferee to be for the personal benefit of the fiduciary, the creditor or other transferee is liable to the principal if the fiduciary in fact commits a breach of his obligation as fiduciary in transferring the instrument. (1923, c. 85, s. 4; C.S., s. 1864(h).)

§ 32-6. Check drawn by fiduciary payable to third person.

If a check or other bill of exchange is drawn by a fiduciary as such, or in the name of his principal by a fiduciary empowered to draw such instrument in the name of his principal, the payee is not bound to inquire whether the fiduciary is committing a breach of his obligation as fiduciary in drawing or delivering the instrument, and is not chargeable with notice that the fiduciary is committing a breach of his obligation as fiduciary unless he takes the instrument with actual knowledge of such breach or with knowledge of such facts that his action in taking the instrument amounts to bad faith. If, however, such instrument is payable to a personal creditor of the fiduciary and delivered to the creditor in payment of or as security for a personal debt of the fiduciary to the actual knowledge of the creditor, or is drawn and delivered in any transaction known by the payee to be for the personal benefit of the fiduciary, the creditor or other payee is liable to the principal if the fiduciary in fact commits a breach of his obligation as fiduciary in drawing or delivering the instrument. (1923, c. 85, s. 5; C.S., s. 1864(i).)

§ 32-7. Check drawn by and payable to fiduciary.

If a check or other bill of exchange is drawn by a fiduciary as such or in the name of his principal by a fiduciary empowered to draw such instrument in the name of his principal, payable to the fiduciary personally, or payable to a third person and by him transferred to the fiduciary, and is thereafter transferred by the fiduciary, whether in payment of a personal debt of the fiduciary or otherwise, the transferee is not bound to inquire whether the fiduciary is committing a breach of his obligation as fiduciary in transferring the instrument, and is not chargeable with notice that the fiduciary is committing a breach of his obligation as fiduciary unless he takes the instrument with actual knowledge of such breach or with knowledge of such facts that his action in taking the instrument amounts to bad faith. (1923, c. 85, s. 6; C.S., s. 1864(j).)

§ 32-8. Deposit in name of fiduciary as such.

If a deposit is made in a bank to the credit of a fiduciary as such, the bank is authorized to pay the amount of the deposit or any part thereof upon the check of the fiduciary, signed with the name in which such deposit is entered, without being liable to the principal, unless the bank pays the check with actual knowledge that the fiduciary is committing a breach of his obligation as fiduciary in drawing the check or with knowledge of such facts that its action in paying the check amounts to bad faith.

If, however, such a check is payable to the drawee bank and is delivered to it in payment of or as security for a personal debt of the fiduciary to it, the bank is liable to the principal if the fiduciary in fact commits a breach of his obligation as fiduciary in drawing or delivering the check. (1923, c. 85, s. 7; C.S., s. 1864(k).)

§ 32-9. Deposit in name of principal.

If a check is drawn upon the account of his principal in a bank by a fiduciary who is empowered to draw checks upon his principal's account, the bank is authorized to pay such check without being liable to the principal, unless the bank pays the check with actual knowledge that the fiduciary is committing a breach of his obligation as fiduciary in drawing such check, or with knowledge of such facts that its action in paying the check amounts to bad faith. If, however, such a check is payable to the drawee bank and is delivered to it in payment of or as security for a personal debt of the fiduciary to it, the bank is liable to the principal if the fiduciary in fact commits a breach of his obligation as fiduciary in drawing or delivering the check. (1923, c. 85, s. 8; C.S., s. 1864(l).)

§ 32-10. Deposit in fiduciary's personal account.

If a fiduciary makes a deposit in a bank to his personal credit of checks drawn by him upon an account in his own name as fiduciary or of checks payable to him as fiduciary or of checks drawn by him upon an account in the name of his principal if he is empowered to draw checks thereon, or checks payable to his principal and indorsed by him, if he is empowered to indorse such checks, or if he otherwise makes a deposit of funds held by him as fiduciary, the bank receiving such deposit is not bound to inquire whether the fiduciary is committing thereby a breach of his obligation as fiduciary; and the bank is authorized to pay the amount of the deposit or any part thereof upon the personal check of the fiduciary without being liable to the principal, unless the bank receives the deposit or pays the check with actual knowledge that the fiduciary is committing a breach of his obligation as fiduciary in making such deposit or in drawing such check, or with knowledge of such facts that its action in receiving the deposit or paying the check amounts to bad faith. (1923, c. 85, s. 9; C.S., s. 1864(m).)

§ 32-11. Deposit in names of two or more trustees.

When a deposit is made in a bank in the name of two or more persons as trustees and a check is drawn upon the trust account by any trustee or trustees authorized by the other trustee or trustees to draw checks upon the trust account, neither the payee nor other holder nor the bank is bound to inquire whether it is a breach of trust to authorize such trustee or trustees to draw checks upon the trust account, and is not liable unless the circumstances be such that the action of the payee or other holder or the bank amounts to bad faith. (1923, c. 85, s. 10; C.S., s. 1864(n).)

§ 32-12. Cases not provided for in Article.

In any case not provided for in this Article the rules of law and equity, including the law merchant and those rules of law and equity relating to trusts, agency, negotiable instruments and banking, shall continue to apply. (1923, c. 85, s. 12; C.S., s. 1864(p); 1965, c. 628, s. 2.)

§ 32-13. Uniformity of interpretation.

This Article shall be so interpreted and construed as to effectuate its general purpose to make uniform the law of those states which enact it. (1923, c. 85, s. 13; C.S., s. 1864(q); 1965, c. 628, s. 2.)

Article 2.

Security Transfers.

§§ 32-14 through 32-24: Repealed by Session Laws 1997-181, s. 23.

Article 3.

Powers of Fiduciaries.

§ 32-25. Definition.

As used in this Article, the term "fiduciary" means the one or more executors of the estate of a decedent, or the one or more trustees of a testamentary or inter vivos trust estate, whichever in a particular case shall be appropriate. (1965, c. 628, s. 1.)

Article 3.

Powers of Fiduciaries.

§ 32-26. Incorporation by reference of powers enumerated in § 32-27; restriction on exercise of such powers.

(a) By an express intention of the testator or settlor so to do contained in a will, or in an instrument in writing whereby a trust estate is created inter vivos, any or all of the powers or any portion thereof enumerated in G.S. 32-27, as they exist at the time of the signing of the will by the testator or at the time of the signing by the first settlor who signs the trust instrument, may be, by appropriate reference made thereto, incorporated in such will or other written instrument, with the same effect as though such language were set forth verbatim in the instrument. Incorporation of one or more of the powers contained in G.S. 32-27 by reference to that section shall be in addition to and not in limitation of the common law or statutory powers of the fiduciary.

(b) No power of authority conferred upon a fiduciary as provided in this Article shall be exercised by such fiduciary in such a manner as, in the aggregate, to deprive the trust or the estate involved of an otherwise available tax exemption, deduction or credit, expressly including the marital deduction, or operate to impose a tax upon a donor or testator or other person as owner of any portion of the trust or estate involved. "Tax" includes, but is not limited to, any federal, State, or local income, gift, estate or inheritance tax.

(c) Nothing herein shall be construed to prevent the incorporation of the powers enumerated in G.S. 32-27 in any other kind of instrument or agreement. (1965, c. 628, s. 1.)

§ 32-27. Powers which may be incorporated by reference in trust instrument. The following powers may be incorporated by reference as provided in G.S. 32-26:

(1) Retain Original Property. - To retain for such time as the fiduciary shall deem advisable any property, real or personal, which the fiduciary may receive, even though the retention of such property by reason of its character, amount, proportion to the total estate or otherwise would not be appropriate for the fiduciary apart from this provision.

(2) Sell and Exchange Property. - To sell, exchange, give options upon, partition or otherwise dispose of any property or interest therein which the fiduciary may hold from time to time, with or without order of court, at public or private sale or otherwise, upon such terms and conditions, including credit, and for such consideration as the fiduciary shall deem advisable, and to transfer and convey the property or interest therein which is at the disposal of the fiduciary, in fee simple absolute or otherwise, free of all trust; and the party dealing with the fiduciary shall not be under a duty to follow the proceeds or other consideration received by the fiduciary from such sale or exchange.

(3) Invest and Reinvest. - To invest and reinvest, as the fiduciary shall deem advisable, in stocks (common or preferred), bonds, debentures, notes, mortgages or other securities, in or outside the United States; in insurance contracts on the life of any beneficiary or of any person in whom a beneficiary has an insurable interest, or in annuity contracts for any beneficiary, in any real or personal property, in investment trusts; in participations in common trust funds, and generally in such property as the fiduciary shall deem advisable,

even though such investment shall not be of the character approved by applicable law but for this provision.

(4)   Invest without Diversification. - To make investments which cause a greater proportion of the total property held by the fiduciary to be invested in investments of one type or of one company than would be considered appropriate for the fiduciary apart from this provision.

(5)   Continue Business. - To the extent and upon such terms and conditions and for such periods of time as the fiduciary shall deem necessary or advisable, to continue or participate in the operation of any business or other enterprise, whatever its form of organization, including but not limited to the power:

a.   To effect incorporation, dissolution, or other change in the form of the organization of the business or enterprise;

b.   To dispose of any interest therein or acquire the interest of others therein;

c.   To contribute thereto or invest therein additional capital or to lend money thereto, in any such case upon such terms and conditions as the fiduciary shall approve from time to time;

d.   To determine whether the liabilities incurred in the conduct of the business are to be chargeable solely to the part of the estate or trust set aside for use in the business or to the estate or trust as a whole; and

e.   In all cases in which the fiduciary is required to file accounts in any court or in any other public office, it shall not be necessary to itemize receipts and disbursements and distributions of property but it shall be sufficient for the fiduciary to show in the account a single figure or consolidation of figures, and the fiduciary shall be permitted to account for money and property received from the business and any payments made to the business in lump sum without itemization.

(6)   Form Corporation or Other Entity. - To form a corporation or other entity and to transfer, assign, and convey to such corporation or entity all or any part of the estate or of any trust property in exchange for the stock, securities or obligations of any such corporation or entity, and to continue to hold such stock and securities and obligations.

(7) Operate Farm. - To continue any farming operation received by the fiduciary pursuant to the will or other instrument and to do any and all things deemed advisable by the fiduciary in the management and maintenance of such farm and the production and marketing of crops and dairy, poultry, livestock, orchard and forest products including but not limited to the following powers:

a. To operate the farm with hired labor, tenants or sharecroppers;

b. To lease or rent the farm for cash or for a share of the crops;

c. To purchase or otherwise acquire farm machinery and equipment and livestock;

d. To construct, repair, and improve farm buildings of all kinds needed in the fiduciary's judgment, for the operation of the farm;

e. To make or obtain loans or advances at the prevailing rate or rates of interest for farm purposes such as for production, harvesting, or marketing, or for the construction, repair, or improvement of farm buildings, or for the purchase of farm machinery or equipment or livestock;

f. To employ approved soil conservation practices in order to conserve, improve, and maintain the fertility and productivity of the soil;

g. To protect, manage and improve the timber and forest on the farm and sell the timber and forest products when it is to the best interest of the estate;

h. To ditch, dam and drain damp or wet fields and areas of the farm when and where needed;

i. To engage in the production of livestock, poultry or dairy products, and to construct such fences and buildings and plant such pastures and crops as may be necessary to carry on such operations;

j. To market the products of the farm; and

k. In general, to employ good husbandry in the farming operation.

(8) Manage Real Property. -

a. To improve, manage, protect, and subdivide any real property;

b. To dedicate or withdraw from dedication parks, streets, highways, or alleys;

c. To terminate any subdivision or part thereof;

d. To borrow money for the purposes authorized by this subdivision for such periods of time and upon such terms and conditions as to rates, maturities and renewals as the fiduciary shall deem advisable and to mortgage or otherwise encumber any such property or part thereof, whether in possession or reversion;

e. To lease any such property or part thereof to commence at the present or in the future, upon such terms and conditions, including options to renew or purchase, and for such period or periods of time as the fiduciary deems advisable although such period or periods may extend beyond the duration of the trust or the administration of the estate involved;

f. To make gravel, sand, oil, gas and other mineral leases, contracts, licenses, conveyances or grants of every nature and kind which are lawful in the jurisdiction in which such property lies;

g. To manage and improve timber and forests on such property, to sell the timber and forest products, and to make grants, leases, and contracts with respect thereto;

h. To modify, renew or extend leases;

i. To employ agents to rent and collect rents;

j. To create easements and release, convey, or assign any right, title, or interest with respect to any easement on such property or part thereof;

k. To erect, repair or renovate any building or other improvement on such property, and to remove or demolish any building or other improvement in whole or in part; and

l. To deal with any such property and every part thereof in all other ways and for such other purposes or considerations as it would be lawful for any person owning the same to deal with such property either in the same or in different ways from those specified elsewhere in this subdivision (8).

(8a) Comply with environmental law. -

a. To inspect property held by the fiduciary, including interests in sole proprietorships, partnerships, or corporations and any assets owned by any such business enterprise, for the purpose of determining compliance with environmental law affecting such property and to respond to any actual or threatened violation of any environmental law affecting property held by the fiduciary;

b. To take, on behalf of the estate or trust, any action necessary to prevent, abate, or otherwise remedy any actual or threatened violation of any environmental law affecting property held by the fiduciary, either before or after the initiation of an enforcement action by any governmental body;

c. To refuse to accept property in trust if the fiduciary determines that any property to be donated to the trust either is contaminated by any hazardous substance or is being used or has been used for any activity directly or indirectly involving hazardous substance which could result in liability to the trust or otherwise impair the value of the assets held therein;

d. To settle or compromise at any time any and all claims against the trust or estate which may be asserted by any governmental body or private party involving the alleged violation of any environmental law affecting property held in trust or in an estate;

e. To disclaim any power granted by any document, statute, or rule of law which, in the sole discretion of the fiduciary, may cause the fiduciary to incur personal liability under any environmental law;

f. To decline to serve as a fiduciary if the fiduciary reasonably believes that there is or may be a conflict of interest between it in its fiduciary capacity and in its individual capacity because of potential claims or liabilities which may be asserted against it on behalf of the trust or estate because of the type or condition of assets held therein.

g. For purposes of this subsection "environmental law" means any federal, state, or local law, rule, regulation, or ordinance relating to protection of the environment or human health. For purposes of this subsection, "hazardous substances" means any substance defined as hazardous or toxic or otherwise regulated by any environmental law. The fiduciary shall be entitled to charge the cost of any inspection, review, abatement, response, cleanup, or remedial action authorized herein against the income or principal of the trust or estate. A fiduciary shall not be personally liable to any beneficiary or other party for any decrease in value of assets in trust or in an estate by reason of the fiduciary's compliance with any environmental law, specifically including any reporting requirement under such law. Neither the acceptance by the fiduciary of property or a failure by the fiduciary to inspect property shall be deemed to create any inference as to whether or not there is or may be any liability under any environmental law with respect to such property.

(9) Pay Taxes and Expenses. - To pay taxes, assessments, compensation of the fiduciary, and other expenses incurred in the collection, care, administration, and protection of the trust or estate.

(10) Receive Additional Property. - To receive additional property from any source and administer such additional property as a portion of the appropriate trust or estate under the management of the fiduciary; provided the fiduciary shall not be required to receive such property without the fiduciary's consent.

(11) Deal with Other Trusts. - In dealing with one or more fiduciaries:

a. To sell property, real or personal, to, or to exchange property with, the trustee of any trust which the decedent or the settlor or his spouse or any child of his shall have created, for such estates and upon such terms and conditions as to sale price, terms of payment, and security as to the fiduciary shall seem advisable; and the fiduciary shall be under no duty to follow the proceeds of any such sale; and

b. To borrow money for such periods of time and upon such terms and conditions as to rates, maturities, renewals and securities as the fiduciary shall deem advisable from any trust created by the decedent, his spouse, or any child of his, for the purpose of paying debts of the decedent, taxes, the costs of the administration of the estate, and like charges against the estate, or any part thereof, or discharging the liability of any fiduciary thereof and to mortgage, pledge or otherwise encumber such portion of the estate or any trust as may be required to secure such loan or loans and to renew such loans.

(12) Borrow Money. - To borrow money for such periods of time and upon such terms and conditions as to rates, maturities, renewals, and security as the fiduciary shall deem advisable, including the power of a corporate fiduciary to borrow from its own banking department, for the purpose of paying debts, taxes,

or other charges against the estate or any trust, or any part thereof, and to mortgage, pledge or otherwise encumber such portion of the estate or any trust as may be required to secure such loan or loans; and to renew existing loans either as maker or endorser.

(13)   Make Advances. - To advance money for the protection of the trust or estate, and for all expenses, losses and liabilities sustained in the administration of the trust or estate or because of the holding or ownership of any trust or estate assets, for which advances with any interest the fiduciary shall have a lien on the assets of the trust or estate as against a beneficiary.

(14)   Vote Shares. - To vote shares of stock owned by the estate or any trust at stockholders meetings in person or by special, limited, or general proxy, with or without power of substitution.

(15)   Register in Name of Nominee. - To hold a security in the name of a nominee or in other form without disclosure of the fiduciary relationship so that title to the security may pass by delivery, but the fiduciary shall be liable for any act of the nominee in connection with the stock so held.

(16)   Exercise Options, Rights, and Privileges. - To exercise all options, rights, and privileges to convert stocks, bonds, debentures, notes, mortgages, or other property into other stocks, bonds, debentures, notes, mortgages, or other property; to subscribe for other or additional stocks, bonds, debentures, notes, mortgages, or other property; and to hold such stocks, bonds, debentures, notes, mortgages, or other property so acquired as investments of the estate or trust so long as the fiduciary shall deem advisable.

(17)   Participate in Reorganizations. - To unite with other owners of property similar to any which may be held at any time in the decedent's estate or in any trusts in carrying out any plan for the consolidation or merger, dissolution or liquidation, foreclosure, lease, or sale of the property, incorporation or reincorporation, reorganization or readjustment of the capital or financial structure of any corporation, company or association the securities of which may form any portion of an estate or trust; to become and serve as a member of a stockholders or bondholders protective committee; to deposit securities in accordance with any plan agreed upon; to pay any assessments, expenses, or sums of money that may be required for the protection or furtherance of the interest of the distributees of an estate or beneficiaries of any trust with reference to any such plan; and to receive as investments of an estate or any trust any securities issued as a result of the execution of such plan.

(18)   Reduce Interest Rates. - To reduce the interest rate from time to time on any obligation, whether secured or unsecured, constituting a part of an estate or trust.

(19)   Renew and Extend Obligations. - To continue any obligation, whether secured or unsecured, upon and after maturity with or without renewal or extension upon such terms as the fiduciary shall deem advisable, without regard to the value of the security, if any, at the time of such continuance.

(20)   Foreclose and Bid in. - To foreclose, as an incident to the collection of any bond, note or other obligation, any mortgage, deed of trust, or other lien securing such bond, note or other obligation, and to bid in the property at such foreclosure sale, or to acquire the property by deed from the mortgagor or obligor without foreclosure; and to retain the property so bid in or taken over without foreclosure.

(21)   Insure. - To carry such insurance coverage, including public liability, for such hazards and in such amounts, either in stock companies or in mutual companies, as the fiduciary shall deem advisable.

(22)   Collect. - To collect, receive, and receipt for rents, issues, profits, and income of an estate or trust.

(23)   Litigate, Compromise or Abandon. - To compromise, adjust, arbitrate, sue on or defend, abandon, or otherwise deal with and settle claims in favor of or against the estate or trust as the fiduciary shall deem advisable, and the fiduciary's decision shall be conclusive between the fiduciary and the beneficiaries of the estate or trust and the person against or for whom the claim is asserted, in the absence of fraud by such persons; and in the absence of fraud, bad faith or gross negligence of the fiduciary, shall be conclusive between the fiduciary and the beneficiaries of the estate or trust.

(24)   Employ and Compensate Agents, etc. - To employ and compensate, out of income or principal or both and in such proportion as the fiduciary shall deem advisable, persons deemed by the fiduciary needful to advise or assist in the proper settlement of the estate or administration of any trust, including, but not limited to, agents, accountants, brokers, attorneys-at-law, attorneys-in-fact, investment brokers, rental agents, realtors, appraisers, and tax specialists; and to do so without liability for any neglect, omission, misconduct, or default of such

agent or representative provided he was selected and retained with due care on the part of the fiduciary.

(25) Acquire and Hold Property of Two or More Trusts Undivided. - To acquire, receive, hold and retain the principal of several trusts created by a single instrument undivided until division shall become necessary in order to make distributions; to hold, manage, invest, reinvest, and account for the several shares or parts of shares by appropriate entries in the fiduciary's books of account, and to allocate to each share or part of share its proportionate part of all receipts and expenses; provided, however, that the provisions of this subdivision shall not defer the vesting in possession of any share or part of share of the estate or trust.

(25a) Divide One Trust into Several Trusts and Make Distributions From Those Trusts. -

a. To divide the funds and properties constituting any trusts into two or more identical separate trusts that represent two or more fractional shares of the funds and properties being divided, or to hold any addition or contribution to an existing trust as a separate, identical trust, and to make distributions of income and principal by a method other than pro rata from the separate trusts so created as the fiduciary determines to be in the best interests of the trust beneficiaries. In any case where two separate, identical trusts are created pursuant to this sub-subdivision, one of which is fully exempt from the federal generation-skipping transfer tax and one of which is fully subject to that tax, the fiduciary may thereafter, to the extent possible consistent with the terms of the governing instrument, determine the value of any mandatory or discretionary distributions to trust beneficiaries on the basis of the combined value of both trusts, but may satisfy such distributions from the separate trusts in a manner designed to minimize the current and potential generation-skipping transfer tax.

b. To divide the funds and properties constituting any trusts into two or more separate, nonidentical trusts if (i) the new trusts so created are not inconsistent with the terms of the governing instrument; and (ii) the terms of the new trusts provide in the aggregate for the same succession of interests and beneficiaries as are provided in the original trust.

c. To fund the new trusts created pursuant to the authority granted under this subdivision either (i) by pro rata allocation of the assets of the original trust; (ii) based upon the fair market value of the assets at the date of division; or (iii) in a manner fairly reflecting the net appreciation or depreciation of the trust assets measured from the valuation date to the date of division.

(25b) Consolidate Similar Trusts. - When the trustee is trustee of more than one trust, the terms of which are substantially similar and the beneficiaries of which are identical, to consolidate the assets of those trusts and administer the assets as one trust under the terms of one of the trusts.

(26) Establish and Maintain Reserves. - To set up proper and reasonable reserves for taxes, assessments, insurance premiums, depreciation, obsolescence, amortization, depletion of mineral or timber properties, repairs, improvements, and general maintenance of buildings or other property out of rents, profits, or other income received; and to set up reserves also for the equalization of payments to or for beneficiaries; provided, however, that the provisions of this subdivision shall not affect the ultimate interests of beneficiaries in such reserves.

(27) Distribute in Cash or Kind. - To make distribution of capital assets of the estate or trust in kind or in cash, or partially in kind and partially in cash, in divided or undivided interests, either pro rata or by a method other than pro rata among all distributees, without regard to the income tax basis or other special tax attributes of such assets, as the fiduciary finds to be most practicable and for the best interests of the distributees; and to determine the value of capital assets for the purpose of making distribution thereof if and when there be more than one distributee thereof, which determination shall be binding upon the distributees unless clearly capricious, erroneous and inequitable; provided, however, that the fiduciary shall not exercise any power under this subdivision unless the fiduciary holds title to or an interest in the property to be distributed and is required or authorized to make distribution thereof.

(28) Pay to or for Minors or Incompetents. - To make payments in money, or in property in lieu of money, to or for a minor or incompetent in any one or more of the following ways:

a. Directly to such minor or incompetent;

b. To apply directly in payment for the support, maintenance, education, and medical, surgical, hospital, or other institutional care of such minor or incompetent;

c. To the legal or natural guardian of such minor or incompetent;

d. To any other person, whether or not appointed guardian of the person by any court, who shall, in fact, have the care and custody of the person of such minor or incompetent.

The fiduciary shall not be under any duty to see to the application of the payments so made, if the fiduciary exercised due care in the selection of the person, including the minor or incompetent, to whom such payments were made; and the receipt of such person shall be full acquittance to the fiduciary.

(28a) Pay to Custodian Under Uniform Gifts or Transfers to Minors Act. - To make any distribution of income or principal, including real property, for the benefit of any distributee to a custodian under the North Carolina Uniform Transfers to Minors Act, Chapter 33A of the General Statutes, or under the provisions of any similar statute in the state where the minor or the custodian resides. Unless a custodian is specifically named in the governing instrument, the fiduciary shall have absolute discretion to nominate any qualified individual or financial institution, including the fiduciary, to serve as custodian, and to nominate one or more substitute custodians.

(29) Apportion and Allocate Receipts and Expenses. - Where not otherwise provided by the Uniform Principal and Income Act of 2003 as contained in Chapter 37A of the General Statutes, to determine:

a. What is principal and what is income of any estate or trust and to allocate or apportion receipts and expenses as between principal and income in the exercise of the fiduciary's discretion, and, by way of illustration and not limitation of the fiduciary's discretion, to charge premiums on securities purchased at a premium against principal or income or partly against each;

b. Whether to apply stock dividends and other noncash dividends to income or principal or apportion them as the fiduciary shall deem advisable; and

c. What expenses, costs, taxes (other than estate, inheritance, and succession taxes and other governmental charges) shall be charged against principal or income or apportioned between principal and income and in what proportions.

(30) Make Contracts and Execute Instruments. - To make contracts and to execute instruments, under seal or otherwise, as may be necessary in the exercise of the powers herein granted.

(31) The foregoing powers shall be limited as follows for any trust which shall be classified as a "private foundation" as that term is defined by section 509 of the Internal Revenue Code of 1954 or corresponding provisions of any subsequent federal tax laws (including each nonexempt charitable trust described in section 4947(a)(1) of the code which is treated as a private foundation) or nonexempt split-interest trust described in section 4947(a)(2) of the Internal Revenue Code of 1954 or corresponding provisions of any subsequent federal tax laws (but only to the extent that section 508(e) of the code is applicable to such nonexempt split-interest trust under section 4947(a)(2)):

a. The fiduciary shall make distributions of such amounts, for each taxable year, at such time and in such manner as not to become subject to the tax imposed by section 4942 of the Internal Revenue Code of 1954, or corresponding provisions of any subsequent federal tax laws.

b. No fiduciary shall engage in any act of self-dealing as defined in section 4941(d) of the Internal Revenue Code of 1954, or corresponding provisions of any subsequent federal tax laws.

c. No fiduciary shall retain any excess business holdings as defined in section 4943(c) of the Internal Revenue Code of 1954, or corresponding provisions of any subsequent federal tax laws.

d. No fiduciary shall make any investments in such manner as to subject the trust to tax under section 4944 of the Internal Revenue Code of 1954, or corresponding provisions of any subsequent federal tax laws.

e. No fiduciary shall make any taxable expenditures as defined in section 4945(d) of the Internal Revenue Code of 1954, or corresponding provisions of any subsequent federal tax laws. (1965, c. 628, s. 1; 1967, c. 24, s. 15; c. 956; 1971, c. 1136, s. 3; 1977, c. 30; 1989, c. 652, s. 20; 1991, c. 192, s. 1; 1995, c. 235, ss. 1-3; 1997-456, s. 27; 1999-144, s. 1; 2003-232, s. 3.)

§ 32-28: Repealed by Session Laws 2005-192, s. 4, effective January 1, 2006.

§§ 32-29 through 32-33. Reserved for future codification purposes.

Article 4.

Restrictions on Exercise of Power for Fiduciary's Benefit.

§ 32-34: Repealed by Session Laws 2005-192, s. 4, effective January 1, 2006.

§§ 32-35 through 32-49. Reserved for future codification purposes.

Article 5.

Compensation.

§§ 32-50 through 32-52: Repealed by Session Laws 2004-139, s. 1, effective January 1, 2005, and applicable to payments made to a fiduciary on or after that date.

Article 6.

Compensation of Trustees and Other Fiduciaries.

§ 32-53. Definitions.

The following definitions apply in this Article:

(1) Legal disability. - A person under a legal disability is a person who is a minor, incompetent, or unborn individual, or whose identity or location is unknown.

(2) Qualified beneficiary. - As defined in G.S. 36C-1-103(15). With respect to a charitable trust defined in G.S. 36C-1-103(4), the term includes (i) a charitable organization described in G.S. 36C-1-110 as having the rights of a qualified beneficiary; or (ii) if there is no such charitable organization, the Attorney General.

(3) Representative. - A person who may represent and bind another as provided in Article 3 of Chapter 36C of the General Statutes, the provisions of which shall apply for purposes of this Article.

(4) Trust. - A trust to which Chapter 36C of the General Statutes applies as provided in G.S. 36C-1-102. (2004-139, s. 2; 2007-106, s. 38.)

§ 32-54. Compensation of trustees.

(a) If the terms of the trust do not specify the trustee's compensation, the trustee is entitled to receive from the assets of the trust compensation that is reasonable under the circumstances.

(b) All of the following factors shall be considered in determining reasonableness of compensation:

(1) The degree of difficulty and novelty of the tasks required of the trustee.

(2) The responsibilities and risks involved.

(3) The amount and character of the trust assets.

(4) The skill, experience, expertise, and facilities of the trustee.

(5) The quality of the trustee's performance.

(6) Comparable charges for similar services.

(7) Time devoted to administering the trust.

(8) Time constraints imposed upon the trustee in administering the trust.

(9) Nature and costs of services delegated to others by the trustee.

(10) Where more than one trustee is serving, the reasonableness of the total fees paid to all trustees.

(11) Other factors which the trustee or the clerk of superior court deems to be relevant. (2004-139, s. 2.)

§ 32-55. Notice.

(a) If the terms of the trust do not specify the trustee's compensation, the trustee may, in the trustee's discretion, give written notice to all qualified beneficiaries of each proposed payment of compensation if the annual amount of compensation exceeds four-tenths of one percent (4/10 of 1%) of the principal value of the assets of the trust on the last day of the trust accounting year.

(b) In lieu of giving written notice of each proposed payment of compensation under subsection (a) of this section, the trustee may give written notice to all qualified beneficiaries of the amount of compensation to be paid to the trustee on a periodic basis or of the method of computation of the compensation. The trustee shall not be required to give additional notice to the qualified beneficiaries unless the amount to be paid to the trustee on a periodic basis or the method of computation of the compensation changes.

(c) If a qualified beneficiary is under a legal disability, notice shall be given to the representative of the beneficiary. If a representative of a qualified beneficiary is not available without court order, notice shall be deemed given under this section if there is at least (i) one qualified beneficiary described in G.S. 36C-1-103(15)a. or b. who is not under a legal disability or a representative of a qualified beneficiary so described; and (ii) one qualified beneficiary described in G.S. 36C-1-103(15)c. who is not under a legal disability or a representative of a qualified beneficiary so described.

(c1) The notice provided for in this section shall contain a statement that the qualified beneficiaries or their representatives to whom the notice is given have 20 days from when notice is given to file a proceeding for review of the reasonableness of the compensation with the clerk of superior court in accordance with Article 2 of Chapter 36C of the General Statutes.

(d) The provisions of G.S. 36C-1-109 regarding notices to persons under Chapter 36C of the General Statutes shall apply for purposes of notices under this Article. (2004-139, s. 2; 2006-259, s. 13(m); 2007-106, s. 39; 2011-339, s. 1.)

§ 32-56. Payment of compensation without court order.

The trustee is authorized to pay the compensation provided for in G.S. 32-54 without prior approval of the clerk of superior court only if:

(1) The annual amount of compensation does not exceed four-tenths of one percent (4/10 of 1%) of the principal value of the assets of the trust on the last day of the trust accounting year; or

(2) Notice has been given pursuant to G.S. 32-55 and no qualified beneficiary or representative of a qualified beneficiary has initiated a proceeding under G.S. 32-57 for review of the reasonableness of the compensation within 20 days after notice has been given by the trustee in accordance with G.S. 32-55. (2004-139, s. 2; 2007-106, s. 40.)

§ 32-57. Judicial review; payment of compensation and other payments with court order.

(a) If the terms of the trust do not specify the trustee's compensation, the trustee or any qualified beneficiary, or representative of a qualified beneficiary, may initiate a proceeding under Article 2 of Chapter 36C of the General Statutes for review of the reasonableness of any compensation or expense reimbursement and for the approval or denial of the payment of compensation or expense reimbursement. A beneficiary may initiate a proceeding even though the 20-day period referred to in G.S. 32-56(2) has expired.

(b) In connection with reviewing the reasonableness of any compensation or expense reimbursement, the clerk of superior court may order the trustee to make appropriate refunds if the clerk determines upon review that a trustee has received excessive compensation or expense reimbursement. (2004-139, s. 2; 2006-259, s. 13(n); 2007-106, s. 41.)

§ 32-58. Reimbursement for expenses incurred.

In addition to the compensation referred to in G.S. 32-54, the trustee shall be entitled to reimbursement out of the assets of the trust for expenses properly incurred or advanced in the administration of the trust and shall be empowered to pay the expenses from the assets of the trust without prior approval of the clerk of superior court. The court may allow reimbursement of other expenses incurred or advanced to which the trustee is entitled in equity and good conscience. The trustee shall have a lien on trust property to secure reimbursement, with reasonable interest, of expenses owed under this section. (2004-139, s. 2; 2007-106, s. 42.)

§ 32-59. Compensation of other fiduciaries.

Unless otherwise provided by the General Statutes or by the instrument creating the fiduciary relationship, fiduciaries other than trustees under a trust shall be entitled, upon written request to the clerk of superior court, to reasonable compensation in an amount to be determined by the clerk after taking into consideration the factors set forth in G.S. 32-54(b) and to reimbursement for expenses properly incurred in the administration of the fiduciary relationship. (2004-139, s. 2.)

§ 32-60. Effect of provisions in instrument.

In those instances where the instrument creating the trust or other fiduciary relationship provides that the compensation of the fiduciary shall be the amount "provided by law", the "maximum amount provided by law", or other similar language, or references former G.S. 32-50, this language shall be construed as an intention that the trustee or other fiduciary shall receive reasonable compensation as allowed under this Article. In those instances where the instrument creating the trust or other fiduciary relationship provides that the trustee or other fiduciary shall serve without compensation, this language shall be construed as being a provision relating to compensation, and the trustee or other fiduciary shall not be entitled to receive reasonable compensation as allowed under this Article. (2004-139, s. 2.)

§ 32-61. Counsel fees allowable to attorneys serving as fiduciaries.

The clerk of superior court may exercise discretion to allow counsel fees to an attorney serving as a fiduciary or trustee (in addition to the compensation allowed to the attorney as a fiduciary or trustee) where the attorney, on behalf of the trust or fiduciary relationship, renders professional services as an attorney that are different from the services normally performed by a fiduciary or trustee and of a type which would reasonably justify the retention of legal counsel by a fiduciary or trustee who is not licensed to practice law. (2004-139, s. 2.)

§ 32-62. Applicability.

Regardless of when the trust or fiduciary relationship is created, the provisions of this Article shall apply to all payments made to a fiduciary after January 1, 2005, including payments for compensation earned prior to January 1, 2005. (2004-139, s. 2.)

§ 32-63. Reserved for future codification purposes.

§ 32-64. Reserved for future codification purposes.

§ 32-65. Reserved for future codification purposes.

§ 32-66. Reserved for future codification purposes.

§ 32-67. Reserved for future codification purposes.

§ 32-68. Reserved for future codification purposes.

§ 32-69. Reserved for future codification purposes.

Article 7.

Investment and Deposit of Trust Funds.

§ 32-70. Definition.

(a) For the purpose of this Article, the word "fiduciary" shall be construed to include a guardian, personal representative, collector, trustee, or any other person charged with the duty of acting for the benefit of another party as to matters coming within the scope of the relationship between them.

(b) As used in subsection (a) above, the word "person" shall be construed to include an individual, a corporation, or any legal or commercial entity authorized to hold property or do business in the State of North Carolina. (1977, c. 502, s. 2; 2005-192, s. 1.)

§ 32-71. Investment; prudent person rule.

(a) In acquiring, investing, reinvesting, exchanging, retaining, selling, and managing property for the benefit of another, a fiduciary shall observe the standard of judgment and care under the circumstances then prevailing, which an ordinarily prudent person of discretion and intelligence, who is a fiduciary of the property of others, would observe as such fiduciary; and if the fiduciary has special skills or is named a fiduciary on the basis of representations of special skills or expertise, he is under a duty to use those skills. This subsection and subsection (b) of this section do not apply to trusts governed by Article 9 of Chapter 36C of the General Statutes.

(b) Within the limitations of the foregoing standard, a fiduciary is authorized to acquire and retain every kind of property and every kind of investment, including specifically, but without in any way limiting the generality of the foregoing, bonds, debentures, and other corporate or governmental obligations; stocks, preferred or common; real estate mortgages; shares in building and loan associations or savings and loan associations; annual premium or single premium life, endowment, or annuity contracts; and securities of any management type investment company or investment trust registered under the Federal Investment Company Act of 1940, as from time to time amended.

(c),(d) Repealed by Session Laws 2007-106, s. 43, effective October 1, 2007. (1870-1, c. 197; Code, s. 1594; 1885, c. 389; 1889, c. 470; Rev., ss. 1792, 1793; 1917, c. 6, s. 9; c. 67, s. 1; c. 152, s. 7; c. 191, s. 1; c. 269, s. 5; C.S., ss. 4018, 4018(a), 4019; Ex. Sess. 1921, c. 63; 1931, c. 257; 1933, c. 549, s. 1; 1935, c. 449; 1937, c. 14; 1943, c. 96; c. 473, ss. 1-3; 1945, c. 713; 1953, c. 620; 1959, c. 364, s. 2; c. 1015, s. 2; 1969, c. 861; 1971, c. 528, s. 34; c. 864, s. 17; 1973, c. 239, s. 1; 1975, cc. 40, 319; 1977, c. 502, s. 2; 1995, c. 153, s. 1; 1999-215, s. 2; 2005-192, s. 1; 2006-259, s. 13(o); 2007-106, s. 43.)

§ 32-72. Terms of creating instrument.

(a) Nothing contained in this Article shall be construed as authorizing any departure from the express terms or limitations set forth in any will, agreement, court order, or other instrument creating or defining the fiduciary's powers and duties.

(b) A fiduciary holding funds for investment who is specifically directed or authorized by an instrument creating the fiduciary relationship to retain the stock of a bank or trust company that is a member of a bank holding company currently fully registered under an act of Congress entitled Bank Holding Company Act of 1956, as the same may be amended from time to time, shall be considered as being directed or authorized to retain the stock of such bank holding company.

(c) Whenever a fiduciary holding funds for investment is directed, required, authorized, or permitted by an instrument creating the fiduciary relationship to invest in United States government obligations, the fiduciary may, in the absence of an express prohibition in the instrument, invest in and hold such obligations either directly or in the form of interests in a money market mutual fund registered under the Investment Company Act of 1940, 15 U.S.C. §§ 80a-1, et seq., as from time to time amended, the portfolio of which is limited to United States government obligations and repurchase agreements fully collateralized thereby.

(d) The following provisions apply to an instrument creating a fiduciary relationship other than a trust instrument to which Chapter 36C of the General Statutes applies and to a fiduciary other than a trustee:

(1) The terms of the instrument may confer upon a person certain powers with respect to the actions of a fiduciary, including, but not limited to, the following:

a. Investments, including retention, purchase, sale, exchange, or other transaction affecting the ownership of investments with respect to all or any one or more assets.

b. Any other matter.

(2) When the terms of the instrument confer upon a person any power with respect to the actions of a fiduciary, the duty and liability of the fiduciary are as follows:

a. If the terms of the instrument confer upon the person the power to direct certain actions of the fiduciary, the fiduciary must act in accordance with the direction and is not liable, individually or as a fiduciary, for any loss resulting directly or indirectly from compliance with the direction unless compliance with the direction constitutes intentional misconduct on the part of the fiduciary.

b. If the terms of the instrument confer upon a person the power to consent to certain actions of the fiduciary, and the power holder does not provide consent within a reasonable time after the fiduciary has made a timely request for the power holder's consent, the fiduciary is not liable, individually or as a fiduciary, for any loss resulting directly or indirectly from the fiduciary's failure to take any action that required the power holder's consent.

b1. If the terms of the instrument confer upon a person a power other than the power to direct or consent to actions of the fiduciary, the fiduciary is not liable, individually or as a fiduciary, for any loss resulting directly or indirectly from the exercise or nonexercise of the power.

c. The fiduciary has no duty to monitor the conduct of the power holder, provide advice to the power holder, or consult with the power holder. The fiduciary is not required to give notice to any beneficiary of any action taken or not taken by the power holder whether or not the fiduciary agrees with the result. Administrative actions taken by the fiduciary for the purpose of implementing directions of the power holder, including confirming that the directions of the power holder have been carried out, do not constitute monitoring of the power holder or other participation in decisions within the scope of the power holder's authority.

(3) A person who holds a power with respect to the actions of a fiduciary is a fiduciary who, as such, is required to act in good faith with regard to the purposes of the estate, or other relationship between the fiduciary and beneficiaries, and the interests of the beneficiaries, except that if a beneficiary is a person with such a power with respect to the actions of a fiduciary, the beneficiary is not a fiduciary with respect to the following:

a. A power that constitutes a power of appointment held by a beneficiary under the instrument.

b. A power the exercise or nonexercise of which affects only the interests of the beneficiary holding the power and no other beneficiary.

c. A power to remove and appoint a fiduciary.

The holder of the power with respect to the actions of a fiduciary is liable for any loss that results from breach of a fiduciary duty occurring as a result of the exercise or nonexercise of the power. (1973, c. 1277; 1977, c. 502, s. 2; 1985, c. 538, s. 1; 2001-413, s. 4; 2005-192, s. 1; 2012-18, s. 3.3; 2013-91, s. 3(b).)

§ 32-73. Power of court not restricted.

Nothing contained in this Article shall be construed as restricting the power of a court of proper jurisdiction to permit a fiduciary to deviate from the terms of any will, agreement, or other instrument relating to the acquisition, investment, reinvestment, exchange, retention, sale, or management of fiduciary property. (1977, c. 502, s. 2; 2005-192, s. 1.)

§ 32-74. Applicability of provisions.

This Article shall govern fiduciaries acting under wills, agreements, court orders, and other instruments now existing or hereafter made. (1977, c. 502, s. 2; 2005-192, s. 1.)

§ 32-75. Employee trusts.

Pension, profit sharing, stock bonus, annuity, or other employee trusts established for the purpose of distributing the income and principal thereof to some or all of their employees, or the beneficiaries of such employees, shall not be invalid as violating any laws or rules against perpetuities, restraints on the power of alienation of title to property, or the accumulation of income; but such trusts may continue for such period of time as may be required by the provisions thereof to accomplish the purpose for which they were established. (1954, c. 8; 1977, c. 502, s. 2; 2005-192, s. 1.)

§ 32-76. Applicability.

The provisions of this Article shall apply to fiduciary relationships in existence on January 1, 1978, or thereafter established. (1977, c. 502, s. 2; 2005-192, s. 1.)

Chapter 32A.

Powers of Attorney.

Article 1.

Statutory Short Form Power of Attorney.

§ 32A-1. Statutory Short Form of General Power of Attorney.

The use of the following form in the creation of a power of attorney is lawful, and, when used, it shall be construed in accordance with the provisions of this Chapter.

"NOTICE: THE POWERS GRANTED BY THIS DOCUMENT ARE BROAD AND SWEEPING. THEY ARE DEFINED IN CHAPTER 32A OF THE NORTH CAROLINA GENERAL STATUTES WHICH EXPRESSLY PERMITS THE USE OF ANY OTHER OR DIFFERENT FORM OF POWER OF ATTORNEY DESIRED BY THE PARTIES CONCERNED.

State of _____.

County of _____.

I _____, appoint _____ to be my attorney-in-fact, to act in my name in any way which I could act for myself, with respect to the following matters as each of them is defined in Chapter 32A of the North Carolina General Statutes. (DIRECTIONS: Initial the line opposite any one or more of the subdivisions as to which the principal desires to give the attorney-in-fact authority.)

(1)....... Real property transactions..
_____

(2)....... Personal property transactions...
_____

(3)....... Bond, share, stock, securities and commodity transactions................
_____

(4)....... Banking transactions..
_____

(5)....... Safe deposits...
_____

(6)....... Business operating transactions..
_____

(7)....... Insurance transactions..
_____

(8)....... Estate transactions..
_____

(9)....... Personal relationships and affairs...

_____

(10)..... Social security and unemployment...

_____

(11)..... Benefits from military service..

_____

(12)..... Tax matters...

_____

(13)..... Employment of agents...

_____

(14)..... Gifts to charities, and to individuals other than the

.... attorney-in-fact..

_____

(15)..... Gifts to the named attorney-in-fact...

_____

(16)..... Renunciation of an interest in or power over property to

.... benefit persons other than the attorney-in-fact...................................

_____

(17)..... Renunciation of an interest in or power over property

.... to benefit persons including the attorney-in-fact................................

_____

(If power of substitution and revocation is to be given, add: 'I also give to such person full power to appoint another to act as my attorney-in-fact and full power to revoke such appointment.')

(If period of power of attorney is to be limited, add: "This power terminates ____, ____')

(If power of attorney is to be a durable power of attorney under the provision of Article 2 of Chapter 32A and is to continue in effect after the incapacity or mental incompetence of the principal, add: 'This power of attorney shall not be affected by my subsequent incapacity or mental incompetence.')

(If power of attorney is to take effect only after the incapacity or mental incompetence of the principal, add: 'This power of attorney shall become effective after I become incapacitated or mentally incompetent.')

(If power of attorney is to be effective to terminate or direct the administration of a custodial trust created under the Uniform Custodial Trust Act, add: 'In the event of my subsequent incapacity or mental incompetence, the attorney-in-fact of this power of attorney shall have the power to terminate or to direct the administration of any custodial trust of which I am the beneficiary.')

(If power of attorney is to be effective to determine whether a beneficiary under the Uniform Custodial Trust Act is incapacitated or ceases to be incapacitated, add: 'The attorney-in-fact of this power of attorney shall have the power to determine whether I am incapacitated or whether my incapacity has ceased for the purposes of any custodial trust of which I am the beneficiary.')

Dated_____, _____ .

_____ (Seal)

Signature

STATE OF _____ COUNTY OF _____

On this _____ day of_____, _____, personally appeared before me, the said named _____ to me known and known to me to be the person described in and who executed the foregoing instrument and he (or she) acknowledged that he (or she) executed the same and being duly sworn by me, made oath that the statements in the foregoing instrument are true.

My Commission Expires _____.

_____

(Signature of Notary Public)

Notary Public (Official Seal)"

(1983, c. 626, s. 1; 1985, c. 162, s. 1; c. 618, s. 1; 1995, c. 331, s. 1; c. 486, s. 2; 2009-48, s. 11.)

§ 32A-2. Powers conferred by the Statutory Short Form Power of Attorney set out in G.S. 32A-1.

The Statutory Short Form Power of Attorney set out in G.S. 32A-1 confers the following powers on the attorney-in-fact named therein:

(1) Real Property Transactions. - To lease, purchase, exchange, and acquire, and to agree, bargain, and contract for the lease, purchase, exchange, and acquisition of, and to accept, take, receive, and possess any interest in real property whatsoever, on such terms and conditions, and under such covenants, as said attorney-in-fact shall deem proper; and to maintain, repair, improve, manage, insure, rent, lease, sell, convey, subject to liens, mortgage, subject to deeds of trust, and in any way or manner deal with all or any part of any interest in real property whatsoever, that the principal owns at the time of execution or may thereafter acquire, for under such terms and conditions, and under such covenants, as said attorney-in-fact shall deem proper.

(2) Personal Property Transactions. - To lease, purchase, exchange, and acquire, and to agree, bargain, and contract for the lease, purchase, exchange, and acquisition of, and to accept, take, receive, and possess any personal property whatsoever, tangible or intangible, or interest thereto, on such terms and conditions, and under such covenants, as said attorney-in-fact shall deem proper; and to maintain, repair, improve, manage, insure, rent, lease, sell, convey, subject to liens and mortgages, and hypothecate, and in any way or manner deal with all or any part of any personal property whatsoever, tangible or intangible, or any interest therein, that the principal owns at the time of execution or may thereafter acquire, under such terms and conditions, and under such covenants, as said attorney-in-fact shall deem proper.

(3) Bond, Share, Stock, Securities and Commodity Transactions. - To request, ask, demand, sue for, recover, collect, receive, and hold and possess

any bond, share, instrument of similar character, commodity interest or any instrument with respect thereto together with the interest, dividends, proceeds, or other distributions connected therewith, as now are, or shall hereafter become, owned by, or due, owing payable, or belonging to, the principal at the time of execution or in which the principal may thereafter acquire interest, to have, use, and take all lawful means and equitable and legal remedies, procedures, and writs in the name of the principal for the collection and recovery thereof, and to adjust, sell, compromise, and agree for the same, and to make, execute, and deliver for the principal, all endorsements, acquittances, releases, receipts, or other sufficient discharges for the same.

(4)   Banking Transaction. - To make, receive, sign, endorse, execute, acknowledge, deliver, and possess checks, drafts, bills of exchange, letters of credit, notes, stock certificates, withdrawal receipts and deposit instruments relating to accounts or deposits in, or certificates of deposit of, banks, savings and loan or other institutions or associations for the principal.

(5)   Safe Deposits. - To have free access at any time or times to any safe deposit box or vault to which the principal might have access as lessee or owner.

(6)   Business Operating Transactions. - To conduct, engage in, and transact any and all lawful business of whatever nature or kind for the principal.

(7)   Insurance Transactions. - To exercise or perform any act, power, duty, right or obligation whatsoever in regard to any contract of life, accident, health, disability or liability insurance or any combination of such insurance procured by or on behalf of the principal prior to execution; and to procure new, different or additional contracts of insurance for the principal and to designate the beneficiary of any such contract of insurance, provided, however, that the agent himself cannot be such beneficiary unless the agent is spouse, child, grandchild, parent, brother or sister of the principal.

(8)   Estate Transactions. - To request, ask, demand, sue for, recover, collect, receive, and hold and possess all devises, as are, owned by, or due, owing, payable, or belonging to, the principal at the time of execution or in which the principal may thereafter acquire interest, to have, use, and take all lawful means and equitable and legal remedies, procedures, and writs in the name of the principal for the collection and recovery thereof, and to adjust, sell, compromise, and agree for the same, and to make, execute, and deliver for the

principal, all endorsements, acquittances, releases, receipts, or other sufficient discharges for the same.

(9) Personal Relationships and Affairs. - To do all acts necessary for maintaining the customary standard of living of the principal, the spouse and children, and other dependents of the principal; to provide medical, dental and surgical care, hospitalization and custodial care for the principal, the spouse, and children, and other dependents of the principal; to continue whatever provision has been made by the principal, for the principal, the spouse, and children, and other dependents of the principal, with respect to automobiles, or other means of transportation; to continue whatever charge accounts have been operated by the principal, for the convenience of the principal, the spouse, and children, and other dependents of the principal, to open such new accounts as the attorney-in-fact shall think to be desirable for the accomplishment of any of the purposes enumerated in this section, and to pay the items charged on such accounts by any person authorized or permitted by the principal or the attorney-in-fact to make such charges; to continue the discharge of any services or duties assumed by the principal, to any parent, relative or friend of the principal; to continue payments incidental to the membership or affiliation of the principal in any church, club, society, order or other organization, or to continue contributions thereto.

In the event the attorney-in-fact named pursuant to G.S. 32A-1 makes a decision regarding the health care of the principal that is contradictory to a decision made by a health care agent appointed pursuant to Article 3 of this Chapter, the decision of the health care agent shall overrule the decision of the attorney-in-fact.

(10) Social Security and Unemployment. - To prepare, execute and file all social security, unemployment insurance and information returns required by the laws of the United States, or of any state or subdivision thereof, or of any foreign government.

(11) Benefits from Military Service. - To execute vouchers in the name of the principal for any and all allowances and reimbursements payable by the United States, or subdivision thereof, to the principal, arising from or based upon military service and to receive, to endorse and to collect the proceeds of any check payable to the order of the principal drawn on the treasurer or other fiscal officer or depository of the United States or subdivision thereof; to take possession and to order the removal and shipment, of any property of the principal from any post, warehouse, depot, dock or other place of storage or

safekeeping, either governmental or private, to execute and to deliver any release, voucher, receipt, bill of lading, shipping ticket, certificate or other instrument which the agent shall think to be desirable or necessary for such purpose; to prepare, to file and to prosecute the claim of the principal to any benefit or assistance, financial or otherwise, to which the principal is, or claims to be, entitled, under the provisions of any statute or regulation existing at the creation of the agency or thereafter enacted by the United States or by any state or by any subdivision thereof, or by any foreign government, which benefit or assistance arises from or is based upon military service performed prior to or after execution.

(12) Tax matters. - To prepare, execute, verify and file in the name of the principal and on behalf of the principal any and all types of tax returns, amended returns, declaration of estimated tax, report, protest, application for correction of assessed valuation of real or other property, appeal, brief, claim for refund, or petition, including petition to the Tax Court of the United States, in connection with any tax imposed or proposed to be imposed by any government, or claimed, levied or assessed by any government, and to pay any such tax and to obtain any extension of time for any of the foregoing; to execute waivers or consents agreeing to a later determination and assessment of taxes than is provided by any statute of limitations; to execute waivers of restriction on the assessment and collection of deficiency in any tax; to execute closing agreements and all other documents, instruments and papers relating to any tax liability of any sort; to institute and carry on through counsel any proceeding in connection with determining or contesting any such tax or to recover any tax paid or to resist any claim for additional tax on any proposed assessment or levy thereof; and to enter into any agreements or stipulations for compromise or other adjustments or disposition of any tax.

(13) Employment of Agents. - To employ agents such as legal counsel, accountants or other professional representation as may be appropriate and to grant such agents such powers of attorney or other appropriate authorization as may be required in connection with such representation or by the Internal Revenue Service or other governmental authority.

(14) Gifts to Charities, and to Individuals Other Than the Attorney-In-Fact. -

a. Except as provided in G.S. 32A-2(14)b., to make gifts of any of the principal's property to any individual other than the attorney-in-fact or to any organization described in sections 170(c) and 2522(a) of the Internal Revenue Code or corresponding future provisions of federal tax law, or both, in accordance with the principal's personal history of making or joining in the making of lifetime gifts. As used in this subdivision "Internal Revenue Code" means the "Code" as defined in G.S. 105-228.90.

b. Except as provided in G.S. 32A-2(14)c., or unless gifts are expressly authorized by the power of attorney under G.S. 32A-2(15), a power described in G.S. 32A-2(14)a. may not be exercised by the attorney-in-fact in favor of the attorney-in-fact or the estate, creditors, or creditors of the estate of the attorney-in-fact.

c. If the power described in G.S. 32A-2(14)a. is conferred upon two or more attorneys-in-fact, it may be exercised by the attorney-in-fact or attorneys-in-fact who are not disqualified by G.S. 32A-2(14)b. from exercising the power of appointment as if they were the only attorney-in-fact or attorneys-in-fact.

d. An attorney-in-fact expressly authorized by this section to make gifts of the principal's property may elect to request the clerk of the superior court to issue an order to make a gift of the property of the principal.

(15) Gifts to the Named Attorney-In-Fact. - To make gifts to the attorney-in-fact named in the power of attorney or the estate, creditors, or creditors of the estate of the attorney-in-fact, in accordance with the principal's personal history of making or joining in the making of lifetime gifts.

(16) Renunciation of an interest in or power over property to benefit persons other than the attorney-in-fact. - To renounce, in accordance with Chapter 31B of the General Statutes, an interest in or power over property, including a power of appointment, to benefit persons other than the attorney-in-fact or the estate, creditors, or the creditors of the estate of the attorney-in-fact, or an individual to whom the attorney-in-fact owes a legal obligation of support.

(17) Renunciation of an interest in or power over property to benefit persons including the attorney-in-fact. - To renounce, in accordance with Chapter 31B of the General Statutes, an interest in or power over property, including a power of appointment, to benefit persons including the attorney-in-fact, or the estate, creditors, or the creditors of the estate of the attorney-in-fact, or an individual to whom the attorney-in-fact owes a legal obligation of support. (1983, c. 626, s. 1; 1985, c. 618, s. 2; 1987, c. 77, s. 1; 1991, c. 639, s. 2; 1995, c. 331, ss. 2-4; 1999-385, ss. 1, 2; 2001-413, s. 5.1; 2009-48, s. 12; 2011-284, s. 36.)

§ 32A-3. Provisions not exclusive; reference to Chapter 32B; limitations on authority.

(a) The provisions of this Article are not exclusive and shall not bar the use of any other or different form of power of attorney desired by the parties concerned.

(b) A power of attorney under the provisions of this Article may refer to Chapter 32B as the same is set out in Chapter 626 of the 1983 Session Laws.

(c) Notwithstanding any other provision of this Chapter, no attorney-in-fact may exercise powers described in G.S. 36C-6-602.1(a) to alter the designation of beneficiaries to receive property on the settlor's death under the settlor's existing estate plan. This subsection shall not impair the authority of an attorney-in-fact to make gifts of the principal's property, as provided in Articles 2A and 2B of this Chapter. (1983, c. 626, s. 1; 1985, c. 609, s. 4; 2007-106, s. 1.1.)

§§ 32A-4 through 32A-7. Reserved for future codification purposes.

Article 2.

Durable Power of Attorney.

§ 32A-8. Definition.

A durable power of attorney is a power of attorney by which a principal designates another his attorney-in-fact in writing and the writing contains a statement that it is executed pursuant to the provisions of this Article or the words "This power of attorney shall not be affected by my subsequent incapacity or mental incompetence," or "This power of attorney shall become effective after I become incapacitated or mentally incompetent," or similar words showing the intent of the principal that the authority conferred shall be exercisable notwithstanding the principal's subsequent incapacity or mental incompetence. Unless the durable power of attorney provides otherwise, where the grant of power or authority conferred by a durable power of attorney is effective only upon the principal's subsequent incapacity or mental incompetence, any person to whom such writing is presented, in the absence of actual knowledge to the contrary, shall be entitled to rely on an affidavit, executed by the attorney-in-fact and setting forth that such condition exists, as conclusive proof of such incapacity or mental incompetence, subject to the provisions of G.S. 32A-13. (1983, c. 626, s. 1; 1991, c. 173, s. 1.)

§ 32A-9. Registered durable power of attorney not affected by incapacity or mental incompetence.

(a) All acts done by an attorney-in-fact pursuant to a durable power of attorney during any period of incapacity or mental incompetence of the principal have the same effect and inure to the benefit of and bind the principal and his successors in interest as if the principal were not incapacitated or mentally incompetent if the power of attorney has been registered under the provisions of subsection (b).

(b) No power of attorney executed pursuant to the provisions of this Article shall be valid subsequent to the principal's incapacity or mental incompetence unless it is registered in the office of the register of deeds of that county in this State designated in the power of attorney, or if no place of registration is designated, in the office of the register of deeds of the county in which the principal has his legal residence at the time of such registration or, if the principal has no legal residence in this State at the time of registration or the attorney-in-fact is uncertain as to the principal's residence in this State, in some county in the State in which the principal owns property or the county in which one or more of the attorneys-in-fact reside. A power of attorney executed pursuant to the provision of this Article shall be valid even though the time of such registration is subsequent to the incapacity or mental incompetence of the principal.

(c) Any person dealing in good faith with an attorney-in-fact acting under a power of attorney executed under this Article shall be protected to the full extent of the powers conferred upon such attorney-in-fact, and no person so dealing with such attorney-in-fact shall be responsible for the misapplication of any money or other property paid or transferred to such attorney-in-fact. (1983, c. 626, s. 1; 1987, c. 77, s. 2.)

§ 32A-10. Relation of attorney-in-fact to court-appointed fiduciary.

(a)   If, following execution of a durable power of attorney, a court of the principal's domicile appoints a conservator, guardian of the principal's person or estate, or other fiduciary charged with the management of all of the principal's property or all of his property except specified exclusions, the attorney-in-fact is accountable to the fiduciary as well as to the principal. The fiduciary has the same power to revoke or amend the power of attorney that the principal would have had if he were not incapacitated or mentally incompetent.

(b)   A principal may nominate, by a durable power of attorney, the conservator, guardian of his estate, or guardian of his person for consideration by the court if protective proceedings for the principal's person or estate are thereafter commenced. The court shall make its appointment in accordance with the principal's most recent nomination in a durable power of attorney except for good cause or disqualification. (1983, c. 626, s. 1.)

§ 32A-11. File with clerk, records, inventories, accounts, fees, and commissions.

(a)   Within 30 days after registration of the power of attorney as provided in G.S. 32A-9(b), the attorney-in-fact shall file with the clerk of superior court in the county of such registration a copy of the power of attorney. Every attorney-in-fact acting under a power of attorney under this Article subsequent to the principal's incapacity or mental incompetence shall keep full and accurate records of all transactions in which he acts as agent of the principal and of all property of the principal in his hands and the disposition thereof.

(b)   Any provision in the power of attorney waiving or requiring the rendering of inventories and accounts shall govern, and a power of attorney that waives the requirement to file inventories and accounts need not be filed with the clerk of superior court. Otherwise, subsequent to the principal's incapacity or mental incompetence, the attorney-in-fact shall file in the office of the clerk of the superior court of the county in which the power of attorney is filed, inventories of the property of the principal in his hands and annual and final accounts of the receipt and disposition of property of the principal and of other transactions in behalf of the principal. The power of the clerk to enforce the filing and his duties in respect to audit and recording of such accounts shall be the same as those in respect to the accounts of administrators, but the fees and charges of the clerk shall be computed or fixed only with relation to property of the principal required to be shown in the accounts and inventories. The fees and charges of the clerk shall be paid by the attorney-in-fact out of the principal's money or other property and allowed in his accounts. If the powers of an attorney-in-fact shall terminate for any reason whatever, he, or his executors or administrators, shall have the right to have a judicial settlement of a final account by any procedure available to executors, administrators or guardians.

(c)   In the event that any power of attorney executed pursuant to the provisions of this Article does not contain the amount of compensation that the attorney-in-fact is entitled to receive or the way such compensation is to be determined, and the principal should thereafter become incapacitated or mentally incompetent, then, subsequent to the principal's incapacity or mental incompetence, the attorney-in-fact shall be entitled to receive reasonable compensation as determined by the clerk of superior court after considering the factors set forth in G.S. 32-54(b). (1983, c. 626, s. 1; 2004-139, s. 3.)

§ 32A-12. Appointment, resignation, removal, and substitutions.

(a)   A power of attorney executed under this Article may contain any provisions, not unlawful, relating to the appointment, resignation, removal and substitution of an attorney-in-fact, and to the rights, powers, duties and responsibilities of the attorney-in-fact.

(b)   If all attorneys-in-fact named in the instrument or substituted shall die, or cease to exist, or shall become incapable of acting, and all methods for substitution provided in the instrument have been exhausted, such power of attorney shall cease to be effective. Any substitution by a person authorized to make it shall be in writing signed and acknowledged by such person. Notice of every other substitution shall be in writing and acknowledged by the person substituted. No substitution or notice subsequent to the principal's subsequent incapacity or mental incompetence shall be effective until it has been recorded in the office of the register of deeds of the county in which the power of attorney has been recorded. (1983, c. 626, s. 1.)

§ 32A-13. Revocation.

(a)   Every power of attorney executed pursuant to the provisions of this Article and registered in an office of the register of deeds in this State as provided in G.S. 32A-9(b) shall be revoked by:

(1)   The death of the principal; or

(2)   Registration in the office of the register of deeds where the power of attorney has been registered of an instrument of revocation executed and acknowledged by the principal while he is not incapacitated or mentally incompetent, or by the registration in such office of an instrument of revocation executed by any person or corporation who is given such power of revocation in the power of attorney, or by this Article, with proof of service thereof in either case on the attorney-in-fact in the manner prescribed for service of summons in civil actions.

(b)   Every power of attorney executed pursuant to the provisions of this Article which has not been registered in an office of the register of deeds in this State shall be revoked by:

(1)   The death of the principal;

(2)   Any method provided in the power of attorney;

(3)   Being burnt, torn, canceled, obliterated, or destroyed, with the intent and for the purpose of revoking it, by the principal himself or by another person in his presence and by his direction, while the principal is not incapacitated or mentally incompetent; or

(4)   A subsequent written revocatory document executed and acknowledged in the manner provided herein for the execution of durable powers of attorney by the principal while not incapacitated or mentally incompetent and delivered to the attorney-in-fact in person or to his last known address by certified or registered mail, return receipt requested.

(c)   As to acts undertaken in good faith reliance upon an affidavit executed by the attorney-in-fact stating that he did not have, at the time of exercise of the power, actual knowledge of the termination of the power by revocation pursuant to the provisions of G.S. 32A-13(b) or by the principal's death, such affidavit is conclusive proof of the nonrevocation or nontermination of the power at that time. This section does not affect any provision in a power of attorney for its termination by the expiration of time or occurrence of an event other than an express revocation. (1983, c. 626, s. 1; 1991, c. 173, s. 2.)

§ 32A-14. Powers of attorney executed under the provisions of G.S. 47-115.1; reference to Chapter 32B; limitations on authority.

(a) A power of attorney executed prior to October 1, 1988, pursuant to G.S. 47-115.1 as it existed prior to October 1, 1983, shall be deemed to be a durable power of attorney as defined in G.S. 32A-8.

(b) A power of attorney under the provisions of this Article may refer to Chapter 32B as the same is set out in Chapter 626 of the 1983 Session Laws.

(c) Notwithstanding any other provision of this Chapter, no attorney-in-fact may exercise powers described in G.S. 36C-6-602.1(a) to alter the designation of beneficiaries to receive property on the settlor's death under the settlor's existing estate plan. This subsection shall not impair the authority of an attorney-in-fact to make gifts of the principal's property, as provided in Articles 2A and 2B of this Chapter. (1983, c. 626, s. 1; 1985, c. 609, s. 5; 1989 (Reg. Sess., 1990), c. 992, s. 1; 2007-106, s. 1.2; 2007-484, s. 39.)

Article 2A.

Authority of Attorney-In-Fact to Make Gifts and to Renounce.

§ 32A-14.1. Gifts under power of attorney.

(a) Except as provided in subsection (b) of this section, if any power of attorney authorizes an attorney-in-fact to do, execute, or perform any act that the principal might or could do or evidences the principal's intent to give the attorney-in-fact full power to handle the principal's affairs or deal with the principal's property, the attorney-in-fact shall have the power and authority to make gifts in any amount of any of the principal's property to any individual or to any organization described in sections 170(c) and 2522(a) of the Internal Revenue Code or corresponding future provisions of federal tax law, or both, in accordance with the principal's personal history of making or joining in the making of lifetime gifts. As used in this subsection, "Internal Revenue Code" means the "Code" as defined in G.S. 105-228.90.

(b) Except as provided in subsection (c) of this section, or unless gifts are expressly authorized by the power of attorney, a power described in subsection (a) of this section may not be exercised by the attorney-in-fact in favor of the attorney-in-fact or the estate, creditors, or the creditors of the estate of the attorney-in-fact.

(c) If the power of attorney described in subsection (a) of this section is conferred upon two or more attorneys-in-fact, it may be exercised by the attorney-in-fact or attorneys-in-fact who are not disqualified by subsection (b) of this section from exercising the power of appointment as if they were the only attorney-in-fact or attorneys-in-fact. If the power of attorney described in subsection (a) of this section is conferred upon one attorney-in-fact, the power of attorney may be exercised by the attorney-in-fact in favor of the attorney-in-fact or the estate, creditors, or the creditors of the estate of the attorney-in-fact pursuant to an order issued by the clerk in accordance with the procedures and provisions of Article 2B of this Chapter.

(d) Subsection (a) of this section shall not in any way impair the right, power, or ability of any principal, by express terms in the power of attorney, to authorize or limit the authority of any attorney-in-fact to make gifts of the principal's property.

(e) An attorney-in-fact expressly authorized by this section to make gifts of the principal's property may elect to request that the clerk of the superior court issue an order approving a gift or gifts of the property of the principal.

(f) This section shall apply to all powers of attorney executed prior to, on, or after October 1, 1995. (1995, c. 331, s. 5; 1999-456, s. 2; 2001-413, s. 5.2.)

§ 32A-14.2. Renunciation under power of attorney.

(a) If any power of attorney authorizes an attorney-in-fact to do, execute, or perform any act that the principal might or could do or evidences the principal's intent to give the attorney-in-fact full power to handle the principal's affairs or deal with the principal's property, but does not expressly authorize the attorney-in-fact to renounce an interest in or power over property, the attorney-in-fact shall not have the power or authority to renounce on behalf of the principal pursuant to Chapter 31B of the General Statutes.

(b) Notwithstanding an express grant of general authority to renounce, an attorney-in-fact that is not an ancestor, spouse, or descendant of the principal may not renounce under a power of attorney to create in the attorney-in-fact or the estate, creditors, or the creditors of the estate of the attorney-in-fact, or in an individual to whom the attorney-in-fact owes a legal obligation of support, an interest in or power over the principal's property by reason of a renunciation unless the power of attorney expressly authorizes a renunciation that benefits the attorney-in-fact or the estate, creditors, or the creditors of the estate of the attorney-in-fact, or an individual to whom the attorney-in-fact owes a legal obligation of support. (2009-48, s. 14.)

§ 32A-14.3. Reserved for future codification purposes.

§ 32A-14.4. Reserved for future codification purposes.

§ 32A-14.5. Reserved for future codification purposes.

§ 32A-14.6. Reserved for future codification purposes.

§ 32A-14.7. Reserved for future codification purposes.

§ 32A-14.8. Reserved for future codification purposes.

§ 32A-14.9. Reserved for future codification purposes.

Article 2B.

Gifts Authorized by Court Order.

§ 32A-14.10. Gifts authorized by court order.

An attorney-in-fact, acting under a power of attorney that does not contain the grant of power set out in G.S. 32A-14.1 and does not expressly authorize gifts of the principal's property, may initiate a special proceeding before the clerk of superior court in accordance with the procedures of Article 33 of Chapter 1 of the General Statutes for authority to make gifts of the principal's property to the extent not inconsistent with the express terms of the power of attorney. The principal and any guardian ad litem appointed for the principal are the defendants in a proceeding pursuant to this Article. The clerk may issue an order setting forth the amounts, frequency, recipients, and proportions of any gifts of the principal's property after considering all relevant factors, including, but not limited to: (i) the size of the principal's estate; (ii) the principal's foreseeable obligations; (iii) the principal's foreseeable maintenance needs; (iv) the principal's personal history of making or joining in the making of lifetime gifts; (v) the principal's estate plan; and (vi) the tax effects of the gifts. If there is no appeal from the decision and order of the clerk within the time prescribed by law, the clerk's order shall be submitted to the judge of the superior court and approved by the court before the order becomes effective. (1995, c. 331, s. 5.)

§ 32A-14.11. Appeal; stay effected by appeal.

Any party in interest may appeal from the decision of the clerk to the judge of the superior court. The procedure for appeal is governed by Article 27A of Chapter 1 of the General Statutes. An appeal taken from the decision of the clerk stays the decision and order of the clerk until the cause is heard and determined by the judge upon the appeal taken. (1995, c. 331, s. 5; 1999-216, s. 7.)

§ 32A-14.12. Costs and fees.

All costs and fees arising in connection with a proceeding under this Article shall be assessed the same as costs and fees are assessed in special proceedings governed by Article 33 of Chapter 1 of the General Statutes. (1995, c. 331, s. 5.)

Article 3.

Health Care Powers of Attorney.

§ 32A-15. General purpose of this Article.

(a)   The General Assembly recognizes as a matter of public policy the fundamental right of an individual to control the decisions relating to his or her medical care, and that this right may be exercised on behalf of the individual by an agent chosen by the individual.

(b)   The purpose of this Article is to establish an additional, nonexclusive method for an individual to exercise his or her right to give, withhold, or withdraw consent to medical treatment, including mental health treatment, when the individual lacks sufficient understanding or capacity to make or communicate health care decisions.

(c)   This Article is intended and shall be construed to be consistent with the provisions of Article 23 of Chapter 90 of the General Statutes provided that in the event of a conflict between the provisions of this Article and Article 23 of Chapter 90, the provisions of Article 23 of Chapter 90 control. No conflict between these Chapters exists when either a health care power of attorney or a declaration provides that the declaration is subject to decisions of a health care agent. If no declaration has been executed by the principal as provided in G.S. 90-321 that expressly covers the principal's present condition and if the health care agent has been given the specific authority in a health care power of attorney to authorize the withholding or discontinuing of life-prolonging measures when the principal is in such condition, the measures may be withheld or discontinued as provided in the health care power of attorney upon the direction and under the supervision of the attending physician, as G.S. 90-322 shall not apply in such case. Nothing in this Article shall be construed to authorize any affirmative or deliberate act or omission to end life other than to permit the natural process of dying.

(d) This Article is intended and shall be construed to be consistent with the provisions of Part 3A of Article 16 of Chapter 130A of the General Statutes. In the event of a conflict between the provisions of this Article and Part 3A of Article 16 of Chapter 130A, the provisions of Part 3A of Article 16 of Chapter 130A control. (1991, c. 639, s. 1; 1993, c. 523, s. 1; 1998-198, s. 1; 1998-217, s. 53; 2007-502, s. 1; 2008-153, s. 4.)

§ 32A-16. Definitions.

The following definitions apply in this Article:

(1) Disposition of remains. - The decision to bury or cremate human remains, as human remains are defined in G.S. 90-210.121, and, subject to G.S. 32A-19(b), arrangements relating to burial or cremation.

(1a) Health care. - Any care, treatment, service, or procedure to maintain, diagnose, treat, or provide for the principal's physical or mental health or personal care and comfort including life-prolonging measures. "Health care" includes mental health treatment as defined in subdivision (8) of this section.

(2) Health care agent. - The person appointed as a health care attorney-in-fact.

(3) Health care power of attorney. - A written instrument that substantially meets the requirements of this Article, that is signed in the presence of two qualified witnesses, and acknowledged before a notary public, pursuant to which an attorney-in-fact or agent is appointed to act for the principal in matters relating to the health care of the principal. The notary who takes the acknowledgement may but is not required to be a paid employee of the attending physician or mental health treatment provider, a paid employee of a health facility in which the principal is a patient, or a paid employee of a nursing home or any adult care home in which the principal resides.

(4) Life-prolonging measures. - Medical procedures or interventions which in the judgment of the attending physician would serve only to postpone artificially the moment of death by sustaining, restoring, or supplanting a vital function, including mechanical ventilation, dialysis, antibiotics, artificial nutrition

and hydration, and similar forms of treatment. Life-prolonging measures do not include care necessary to provide comfort or to alleviate pain.

(5) Principal. - The person making the health care power of attorney.

(6) Qualified witness. - A witness in whose presence the principal has executed the health care power of attorney, who believes the principal to be of sound mind, and who states that he or she (i) is not related within the third degree to the principal nor to the principal's spouse, (ii) does not know nor have a reasonable expectation that he or she would be entitled to any portion of the estate of the principal upon the principal's death under any existing will or codicil of the principal or under the Intestate Succession Act as it then provides, (iii) is not the attending physician or mental health treatment provider of the principal, nor a licensed health care provider who is a paid employee of the attending physician or mental health treatment provider, nor a paid employee of a health facility in which the principal is a patient, nor a paid employee of a nursing home or any adult care home in which the principal resides, and (iv) does not have a claim against any portion of the estate of the principal at the time of the principal's execution of the health care power of attorney.

(7) Advance instruction for mental health treatment or advance instruction. - As defined in G.S. 122C-72(1).

(8) Mental health treatment. - The process of providing for the physical, emotional, psychological, and social needs of the principal for the principal's mental illness. "Mental health treatment" includes electroconvulsive treatment, treatment of mental illness with psychotropic medication, and admission to and retention in a facility for care or treatment of mental illness. (1991, c. 639, s. 1; 1998-198, s. 1; 1998-217, s. 53; 2005-351, s. 1; 2006-226, s. 32; 2007-502, s. 2.)

§ 32A-17. Who may make a health care power of attorney.

Any person having understanding and capacity to make and communicate health care decisions, who is 18 years of age or older, may make a health care power of attorney. (1991, c. 639, s. 1.)

§ 32A-18. Who may act as a health care attorney-in-fact.

Any competent person who is not engaged in providing health care to the principal for remuneration, and who is 18 years of age or older, may act as a health care agent. (1991, c. 639, s. 1.)

§ 32A-19. Extent of authority; limitations of authority.

(a)   A principal, pursuant to a health care power of attorney, may grant to the health care agent full power and authority to make health care decisions to the same extent that the principal could make those decisions for himself or herself if he or she had capacity to make and communicate health care decisions, including without limitation, the power to authorize withholding or discontinuing life-prolonging measures and the power to authorize the giving or withholding of mental health treatment. A health care power of attorney may also contain or incorporate by reference any lawful guidelines or directions relating to the health care of the principal as the principal deems appropriate.

(a1)   A health care power of attorney may incorporate or be combined with an advance instruction for mental health treatment prepared pursuant to Part 2 of Article 3 of Chapter 122C of the General Statutes. A health care agent's decisions about mental health treatment shall be consistent with any statements the principal has expressed in an advance instruction for mental health treatment if one so exists, and if none exists, shall be consistent with what the agent believes in good faith to be the manner in which the principal would act if the principal did not lack capacity to make or communicate health care decisions. A health care agent is not subject to criminal prosecution, civil liability, or professional disciplinary action for any action taken in good faith pursuant to an advance instruction for mental health treatment.

(b)   A health care power of attorney may authorize the health care agent to exercise any and all rights the principal may have with respect to anatomical gifts, the authorization of any autopsy, and the disposition of remains; provided this authority is limited to incurring reasonable costs related to exercising these powers, and a health care power of attorney does not give the health care agent general authority over a principal's property or financial affairs.

(c) A health care power of attorney may contain, and the authority of the health care agent shall be subject to, the specific limitations or restrictions as the principal deems appropriate.

(d) The powers and authority granted to the health care agent pursuant to a health care power of attorney shall be limited to the matters addressed in it, and, except as necessary to exercise such powers and authority relating to health care, shall not confer any power or authority with respect to the property or financial affairs of the principal.

(e) This Article shall not be construed to invalidate a power of attorney that authorizes an agent to make health care decisions for the principal, which was executed prior to October 1, 1991.

(f) A health care power of attorney does not limit any authority in Article 5 of Chapter 122C of the General Statutes either to take a person into custody or to admit, retain, or treat a person in a facility. (1991, c. 639, s. 1; 1998-198, s. 1; 1998-217, s. 53; 2007-502, s. 3.)

§ 32A-20. Effectiveness and duration; revocation.

(a) A health care power of attorney shall become effective when and if the physician or physicians or, in the case of mental health treatment, physician or eligible psychologist as defined in G.S. 122C-3(13d), designated by the principal determine in writing that the principal lacks sufficient understanding or capacity to make or communicate decisions relating to the health care of the principal, and shall continue in effect during the incapacity of the principal. The determination shall be made by the principal's attending physician or eligible psychologist if the physician or physicians or eligible psychologist designated by the principal is unavailable or is otherwise unable or unwilling to make this determination or if the principal failed to designate a physician or physicians or eligible psychologist to make this determination. A health care power of attorney may include a provision that, if the principal does not designate a physician for reasons based on his religious or moral beliefs as specified in the health care power of attorney, a person designated by the principal in the health care power of attorney may certify in writing, acknowledged before a notary public, that the principal lacks sufficient understanding or capacity to make or communicate decisions relating to his health care. The person so designated must be a competent person 18 years of age or older, not engaged in providing health care to the principal for remuneration, and must be a person other than the health care agent. For purposes of exercising authority described in G.S. 32A-19(b), however, a health care power of attorney shall be effective following the death of the principal without regard to the principal's understanding or capacity when the principal was living. Nothing in this section shall be construed to prevent a principal from revoking a health care power of attorney.

(b) Except for purposes of exercising authority granted by a health care power of attorney with respect to anatomical gifts, autopsy, or disposition of remains as provided in G.S. 32A-19(b), a health care power of attorney is revoked by the death of the principal. A health care power of attorney may be revoked by the principal at any time, so long as the principal is capable of making and communicating health care decisions. The principal may exercise this right of revocation by executing and acknowledging an instrument of revocation, by executing and acknowledging a subsequent health care power of attorney, or in any other manner by which the principal is able to communicate an intent to revoke. This revocation becomes effective only upon communication by the principal to each health care agent named in the revoked health care power of attorney and to the principal's attending physician or eligible psychologist.

(c) The authority of a health care agent who is the spouse of the principal shall be revoked upon the entry by a court of a decree of divorce or separation between the principal and the health care agent; provided that if the health care power of attorney designates a successor health care agent, the successor shall serve as the health care agent, and the health care power of attorney shall not be revoked. (1991, c. 639, s. 1; 1993, c. 523, s. 2; 1998-198, s. 1; 1998-217, s. 53; 2005-351, s. 2; 2006-226, s. 32; 2011-344, s. 10; 2012-18, s. 3.11.)

§ 32A-21. Appointment, resignation, removal, and substitution.

(a) A health care power of attorney may contain provisions relating to the appointment, resignation, removal and substitution of the health care agent.

(b) If all health care agents named in the instrument or substituted, die or for any reason fail or refuse to act, and all methods of substitution have been exhausted, the health care power of attorney shall cease to be effective. (1991, c. 639, s. 1.)

§ 32A-22. Relation of the health care agent to a court-appointed fiduciary and to a general attorney-in-fact.

(a)   If, following the execution of a health care power of attorney, a court of competent jurisdiction appoints a guardian of the person of the principal, or a general guardian with powers over the person of the principal, the guardian may petition the court, after giving notice to the health care agent, to suspend the authority of the health care agent during the guardianship. The court may suspend the authority of the health care agent for good cause shown, provided that the court's order must direct whether the guardian shall act consistently with the health care power of attorney or whether and in what respect the guardian may deviate from it. Any order suspending the authority of the health care agent must set forth the court's findings of fact and conclusions of law. The guardian shall act consistently with G.S. 35A-1201(a)(5). A health care provider shall be fully protected from liability in relying on a health care power of attorney until given actual notice of the court's order suspending the authority of the health care agent.

(b)   A principal may nominate, by a health care power of attorney, the guardian of the person of the principal if a guardianship proceeding is thereafter commenced. The court shall make its appointment in accordance with the principal's most recent nomination in an unrevoked health care power of attorney, except for good cause shown.

(c)   The execution of a health care power of attorney shall not revoke, restrict or otherwise affect any nonhealth care powers granted by the principal to an attorney-in-fact pursuant to a general power of attorney; provided that the powers granted to the health care agent with respect to health care matters shall be superior to any similar powers granted by the principal to an attorney-in-fact under a general power of attorney.

(d)   A health care power of attorney may be combined with or incorporated into a general power of attorney which is executed in accordance with the requirements of this Article. (1991, c. 639, s. 1; 1998-198, s. 1; 1998-217, s. 53; 2007-502, s. 4.)

§ 32A-23. Article 2, Chapter 32A, not applicable.

The provisions of Article 2 of this Chapter shall not be applicable to a health care power of attorney executed pursuant to this Article. (1991, c. 639, s. 1.)

§ 32A-24. Reliance on health care power of attorney; defense.

(a) Any physician or other health care provider involved in the medical care of the principal may rely upon the authority of the health care agent contained in a signed and acknowledged health care power of attorney in the absence of actual knowledge of revocation of the health care power of attorney. The physician or health care provider may rely upon a copy of the health care power of attorney obtained from the Advance Health Care Directive Registry maintained by the Secretary of State pursuant to Article 21 of Chapter 130A of the General Statutes to the same extent that the individual may rely upon the original document.

(b) All health care decisions made by a health care agent pursuant to a health care power of attorney during any period following a determination that the principal lacks understanding or capacity to make or communicate health care decisions shall have the same effect as if the principal were not incapacitated and were present and acting on his or her own behalf. Any health care provider relying in good faith on the authority of a health care agent shall be protected to the full extent of the power conferred upon the health care agent, and no person so relying on the authority of the health care agent shall be liable, by reason of his reliance, for actions taken pursuant to a decision of the health care agent.

(c) The withholding or withdrawal of life-prolonging measures by or under the orders of a physician pursuant to the authorization of a health care agent shall not be considered suicide or the cause of death for any civil or criminal purpose nor shall it be considered unprofessional conduct or a lack of professional competence. Any person, institution or facility, including without limitation the health care agent and the attending physician, against whom criminal or civil liability is asserted because of conduct described in this section, may interpose this section as a defense.

(d) The protections of this section extend to any valid health care power of attorney, including a document valid under G.S. 32A-27; these protections are not limited to health care powers of attorney prepared in accordance with the statutory form provided in G.S. 32A-25.1, or to health care powers of attorney filed with the Advance Health Care Directive Registry maintained by the Secretary of State. A health care provider may rely in good faith on an oral or written statement by legal counsel that a document appears to meet applicable statutory requirements for a health care power of attorney. These protections also extend to a document executed in another jurisdiction that is valid as a health care power of attorney under G.S. 32A-27. A health care provider shall have no liability for acting in accordance with a revoked health care power of attorney unless that provider has actual notice of the revocation. (1991, c. 639, s. 1; 2001-455, s. 3; 2001-513, s. 30(b); 2007-502, ss. 5(a), (b).)

§ 32A-25: Repealed by Session Laws 2007-502, s. 6(a), effective October 1, 2007.

§ 32A-25.1. Statutory form health care power of attorney.

(a) The use of the following form in the creation of a health care power of attorney is lawful and, when used, it shall meet the requirements of and be construed in accordance with the provisions of this Article:

HEALTH CARE POWER OF ATTORNEY

NOTE: YOU SHOULD USE THIS DOCUMENT TO NAME A PERSON AS YOUR HEALTH CARE AGENT IF YOU ARE COMFORTABLE GIVING THAT PERSON BROAD AND SWEEPING POWERS TO MAKE HEALTH CARE DECISIONS FOR YOU. THERE IS NO LEGAL REQUIREMENT THAT ANYONE EXECUTE A HEALTH CARE POWER OF ATTORNEY.

EXPLANATION: You have the right to name someone to make health care decisions for you when you cannot make or communicate those decisions. This form may be used to create a health care power of attorney, and meets the requirements of North Carolina law. However, you are not required to use this form, and North Carolina law allows the use of other forms that meet certain requirements. If you prepare your own health care power of attorney, you should be very careful to make sure it is consistent with North Carolina law.

This document gives the person you designate as your health care agent broad powers to make health care decisions for you when you cannot make the decision yourself or cannot communicate your decision to other people. You should discuss your wishes concerning life-prolonging measures, mental health treatment, and other health care decisions with your health care agent. Except to the extent that you express specific limitations or restrictions in this form, your health care agent may make any health care decision you could make yourself.

This form does not impose a duty on your health care agent to exercise granted powers, but when a power is exercised, your health care agent will be obligated to use due care to act in your best interests and in accordance with this document.

This Health Care Power of Attorney form is intended to be valid in any jurisdiction in which it is presented, but places outside North Carolina may impose requirements that this form does not meet.

If you want to use this form, you must complete it, sign it, and have your signature witnessed by two qualified witnesses and proved by a notary public. Follow the instructions about which choices you can initial very carefully. Do not sign this form until two witnesses and a notary public are present to watch you sign it. You then should give a copy to your health care agent and to any alternates you name. You should consider filing it with the Advance Health Care Directive Registry maintained by the North Carolina Secretary of State: http://www.nclifelinks.org/ahcdr/

1. Designation of Health Care Agent.

I, _____, being of sound mind, hereby appoint the following person(s) to serve as my health care agent(s) to act for me and in my name (in any way I could act in person) to make health care decisions for me as authorized in this document. My designated health care agent(s) shall serve alone, in the order named.

A. Name: _____   Home Telephone: _____

   Home Address: _____   Work Telephone: _____

   _____ Cellular Telephone: _____

B. Name: _____   Home Telephone: _____

   Home Address: _____   Work Telephone: _____

   _____ Cellular Telephone: _____

C. Name: _____   Home Telephone: _____

   Home Address: _____   Work Telephone: _____

_____   Cellular Telephone:
_____

Any successor health care agent designated shall be vested with the same power and duties as if originally named as my health care agent, and shall serve any time his or her predecessor is not reasonably available or is unwilling or unable to serve in that capacity.

2. Effectiveness of Appointment.

My designation of a health care agent expires only when I revoke it. Absent revocation, the authority granted in this document shall become effective when and if one of the physician(s) listed below determines that I lack capacity to make or communicate decisions relating to my health care, and will continue in effect during that incapacity, or until my death, except if I authorize my health care agent to exercise my rights with respect to anatomical gifts, autopsy, or disposition of my remains, this authority will continue after my death to the extent necessary to exercise that authority.

1. _____ (Physician)

2. _____ (Physician)

If I have not designated a physician, or no physician(s) named above is reasonably available, the determination that I lack capacity to make or communicate decisions relating to my health care shall be made by my attending physician.

3. Revocation.

Any time while I am competent, I may revoke this power of attorney in a writing I sign or by communicating my intent to revoke, in any clear and consistent manner, to my health care agent or my health care provider.

4. General Statement of Authority Granted.

Subject to any restrictions set forth in Section 5 below, I grant to my health care agent full power and authority to make and carry out all health care decisions for me. These decisions include, but are not limited to:

A. Requesting, reviewing, and receiving any information, verbal or written, regarding my physical or mental health, including, but not limited to, medical and hospital records, and to consent to the disclosure of this information.

B. Employing or discharging my health care providers.

C. Consenting to and authorizing my admission to and discharge from a hospital, nursing or convalescent home, hospice, long-term care facility, or other health care facility.

D. Consenting to and authorizing my admission to and retention in a facility for the care or treatment of mental illness.

E. Consenting to and authorizing the administration of medications for mental health treatment and electroconvulsive treatment (ECT) commonly referred to as "shock treatment."

F. Giving consent for, withdrawing consent for, or withholding consent for, X-ray, anesthesia, medication, surgery, and all other diagnostic and treatment procedures ordered by or under the authorization of a licensed physician, dentist, podiatrist, or other health care provider. This authorization specifically includes the power to consent to measures for relief of pain.

G. Authorizing the withholding or withdrawal of life-prolonging measures.

H. Providing my medical information at the request of any individual acting as my attorney-in-fact under a durable power of attorney or as a Trustee or successor Trustee under any Trust Agreement of which I am a Grantor or Trustee, or at the request of any other individual whom my health care agent believes should have such information. I desire that such information be provided whenever it would expedite the prompt and proper handling of my affairs or the affairs of any person or entity for which I have some responsibility. In addition, I authorize my health care agent to take any and all legal steps necessary to ensure compliance with my instructions providing access to my protected health information. Such steps shall include resorting to any and all legal procedures in and out of courts as may be necessary to enforce my rights under the law and shall include attempting to recover attorneys' fees against anyone who does not comply with this health care power of attorney.

I. To the extent I have not already made valid and enforceable arrangements during my lifetime that have not been revoked, exercising any right I may have to authorize an autopsy or direct the disposition of my remains.

J. Taking any lawful actions that may be necessary to carry out these decisions, including, but not limited to: (i) signing, executing, delivering, and acknowledging any agreement, release, authorization, or other document that may be necessary, desirable, convenient, or proper in order to exercise and carry out any of these powers; (ii) granting releases of liability to medical providers or others; and (iii) incurring reasonable costs on my behalf related to exercising these powers, provided that this health care power of attorney shall not give my health care agent general authority over my property or financial affairs.

5. Special Provisions and Limitations.

(Notice: The authority granted in this document is intended to be as broad as possible so that your health care agent will have authority to make any decisions you could make to obtain or terminate any type of health care treatment or service. If you wish to limit the scope of your health care agent's powers, you may do so in this section. If none of the following are initialed, there will be no special limitations on your agent's authority.)

        A. Limitations about Artificial Nutrition or Hydration: In exercising the authority to make health care decisions on my behalf, my health care agent:

_____ shall NOT have the authority to withhold artificial nutrition
  (Initial) (such as through tubes) OR may exercise that authority only
        in accordance with the following special provisions:

_____

_____

_____   shall NOT have the authority to withhold artificial
hydration
    (Initial)   (such as through tubes) OR may exercise that
authority only
                     in accordance with the following special provisions:

_____

_____

NOTE: If you initial either block but do not insert any special provisions, your health care agent shall have NO AUTHORITY to withhold artificial nutrition or hydration.

_____   B.   Limitations Concerning Health Care Decisions. In
exercising
    (Initial)   the authority to make health care decisions on my
behalf, the
                          authority of my health care agent is subject to the
following
                          special provisions: (Here you may include any
specific
                          provisions you deem appropriate such as: your
own definition
                          of when life-prolonging measures should be
withheld or
                          discontinued, or instructions to refuse any specific
types of
                          treatment that are inconsistent with your religious
beliefs, or
                          are unacceptable to you for any other reason.)

_____

_____

NOTE: DO NOT initial unless you insert a limitation.

_____
(Initial)

C. Limitations Concerning Mental Health Decisions. In exercising the authority to make mental health decisions on my behalf, the authority of my health care agent is subject to the following special provisions: (Here you may include any specific provisions you deem appropriate such as: limiting the grant of authority to make only mental health treatment decisions, your own instructions regarding the administration or withholding of psychotropic medications and electroconvulsive treatment (ECT), instructions regarding your admission to and retention in a health care facility for mental health treatment, or instructions to refuse any specific types of treatment that are unacceptable to you.)

_____

_____

NOTE: DO NOT initial unless you insert a limitation.

_____
(Notice:
  (Initial)
or be
health
Article 3 of
may use to

D. Advance Instruction for Mental Health Treatment. This health care power of attorney may incorporate combined with an advance instruction for mental treatment, executed in accordance with Part 2 of Chapter 122C of the General Statutes, which you

_____ treatment in communicate mental care agent's you have indicate here for mental

state your instructions regarding mental health the event you lack capacity to make or health treatment decisions. Because your health decisions must be consistent with any statements expressed in an advance instruction, you should whether you have executed an advance instruction health treatment):

_____

_____

NOTE: DO NOT initial unless you insert a limitation.

_____
   the
    (Initial)   E.   Autopsy and Disposition of Remains. In exercising
 disposition   authority to make decisions regarding autopsy and
 care agent   of remains on my behalf, the authority of my health
 limitations.   is subject to the following special provisions and
 deem   (Here you may include any specific limitations you
 and the   appropriate such as: limiting the grant of authority
 or   scope of authority, or instructions regarding burial
                        cremation):

_____

_____

NOTE: DO NOT initial unless you insert a limitation.

6. Organ Donation.

To the extent I have not already made valid and enforceable arrangements during my lifetime that have not been revoked, my health care agent may exercise any right I may have to:

_____ donate any needed organs or parts; or

(Initial)

_____ donate only the following organs or parts:

(Initial)

_____

NOTE: DO NOT INITIAL BOTH BLOCKS ABOVE.

_____ donate my body for anatomical study if needed.

(Initial)

_____ In exercising the authority to make donations, my health care
(Initial) agent is subject to the following special provisions
and
limitations: (Here you may include any specific
limitations

authority   you deem appropriate such as: limiting the grant of

gifts of   and the scope of authority, or instructions regarding

                    the body or body parts.)

_____

_____

_____

NOTE: DO NOT initial unless you insert a limitation.

NOTE: NO AUTHORITY FOR ORGAN DONATION IS GRANTED IN THIS INSTRUMENT WITHOUT YOUR INITIALS.

7. Guardianship Provision.

If it becomes necessary for a court to appoint a guardian of my person, I nominate the persons designated in Section 1, in the order named, to be the guardian of my person, to serve without bond or security. The guardian shall act consistently with G.S. 35A-1201(a)(5).

8. Reliance of Third Parties on Health Care Agent.

A. No person who relies in good faith upon the authority of or any representations by my health care agent shall be liable to me, my estate, my heirs, successors, assigns, or personal representatives, for actions or omissions in reliance on that authority or those representations.

B.   The powers conferred on my health care agent by this document may be exercised by my health care agent alone, and my health care agent's signature or action taken under the authority granted in this document may be accepted by persons as fully authorized by me and with the same force and effect as if I were personally present, competent, and acting on my own behalf. All acts performed in good faith by my health care agent pursuant to this power of attorney are done with my consent and shall have the same validity and effect as if I were present and exercised the powers myself, and shall inure to the benefit of and bind me, my estate, my heirs, successors, assigns, and personal representatives. The authority of my health care agent pursuant to this power of attorney shall be superior to and binding upon my family, relatives, friends, and others.

9.   Miscellaneous Provisions.

A.   Revocation of Prior Powers of Attorney. I revoke any prior health care power of attorney. The preceding sentence is not intended to revoke any general powers of attorney, some of the provisions of which may relate to health care; however, this power of attorney shall take precedence over any health care provisions in any valid general power of attorney I have not revoked.

B.   Jurisdiction, Severability, and Durability. This Health Care Power of Attorney is intended to be valid in any jurisdiction in which it is presented. The powers delegated under this power of attorney are severable, so that the invalidity of one or more powers shall not affect any others. This power of attorney shall not be affected or revoked by my incapacity or mental incompetence.

C.   Health Care Agent Not Liable. My health care agent and my health care agent's estate, heirs, successors, and assigns are hereby released and forever discharged by me, my estate, my heirs, successors, assigns, and personal representatives from all liability and from all claims or demands of all kinds arising out of my health care agent's acts or omissions, except for my health care agent's willful misconduct or gross negligence.

D. No Civil or Criminal Liability. No act or omission of my health care agent, or of any other person, entity, institution, or facility acting in good faith in reliance on the authority of my health care agent pursuant to this Health Care Power of Attorney shall be considered suicide, nor the cause of my death for any civil or criminal purposes, nor shall it be considered unprofessional conduct or as lack of professional competence. Any person, entity, institution, or facility against whom criminal or civil liability is asserted because of conduct authorized by this Health Care Power of Attorney may interpose this document as a defense.

E. Reimbursement. My health care agent shall be entitled to reimbursement for all reasonable expenses incurred as a result of carrying out any provision of this directive.

By signing here, I indicate that I am mentally alert and competent, fully informed as to the contents of this document, and understand the full import of this grant of powers to my health care agent.

This the _____ day of _____, 20____.

_____(SEAL)

I hereby state that the principal, _____, being of sound mind, signed (or directed another to sign on the principal's behalf) the foregoing health care power of attorney in my presence, and that I am not related to the principal by blood or marriage, and I would not be entitled to any portion of the estate of the principal under any existing will or codicil of the principal or as an heir under the Intestate Succession Act, if the principal died on this date without a will. I also state that I am not the principal's attending physician, nor a licensed health care provider or mental health treatment provider who is (1) an employee of the principal's attending physician or mental health treatment provider, (2) an employee of the health facility in which the principal is a patient, or (3) an employee of a nursing home or any adult care home where the principal resides. I further state that I do not have any claim against the principal or the estate of the principal.

Date: _____   Witness:
_____

Date: _____   Witness:
_____

_____COUNTY, _____STATE

Sworn to (or affirmed) and subscribed before me this day by
_____

                                                                (type/print
name of signer)

_____
                                                                (type/print
name of witness)

_____

(type/print name of witness)

Date: _____

_____

(Official Seal)   Signature of Notary Public

Notary Public

_____,

Printed or typed name

My commission expires:

_____

(b)   Use of the statutory form prescribed in this section is an optional and nonexclusive method for creating a health care power of attorney and does not affect the use of other forms of health care powers of attorney, including previous statutory forms. (1991, c. 639, s. 1; 1993, c. 523, s. 3; 1998-198, s. 1; 1998-217, s. 53; 2005-351, s. 3; 2006-226, s. 32; 2007-502, s. 6(b); 2008-187, s. 37(a).)

§ 32A-26. Health care power of attorney and declaration of desire for natural death.

A health care power of attorney meeting the requirements of this Article may be combined with or incorporated into a Declaration of A Desire For A Natural Death which meets the requirements of Article 23 of Chapter 90 of the General Statutes. (1991, c. 639, s. 1.)

§ 32A-27. Health care powers of attorney executed in other jurisdictions.

Notwithstanding G.S. 32A-16(3), a health care power of attorney or similar document executed in a jurisdiction other than North Carolina shall be valid as a health care power of attorney in this State if it appears to have been executed in accordance with the applicable requirements of that jurisdiction or of this State. (2007-502, s. 7.)

Article 4.

Consent to Health Care for Minor.

§ 32A-28. Purpose.

(a)　　The General Assembly recognizes as a matter of public policy the fundamental right of a parent to delegate decisions relating to health care for the parent's minor child where the parent is unavailable for a period of time by reason of travel or otherwise.

(b)　　The purpose of this Article is to establish a nonexclusive method for a parent to authorize in the parent's absence consent to health care for the parent's minor child. This Article is not intended to be in derogation of the common law or of Article 1A of Chapter 90 of the General Statutes. (1993, c. 150, s. 1.)

§ 32A-29. Definitions.

As used in this Article, unless the context clearly requires otherwise, the term:

(1) "Agent" means the person authorized pursuant to this Article to consent to and authorize health care for a minor child.

(2) "Authorization to consent to health care for minor" means a written instrument, signed by the custodial parent and acknowledged before a notary public, pursuant to which the custodial parent authorizes an agent to authorize and consent to health care for the minor child of the custodial parent, and which substantially meets the requirements of this Article.

(3) "Custodial parent" means a parent having sole or joint legal custody of that parent's minor child.

(4) "Health care" means any care, treatment, service or procedure to maintain, diagnose, treat, or provide for a minor child's physical or mental or personal care and comfort, including life sustaining procedures and dental care.

(5) "Life sustaining procedures" are those forms of care or treatment which only serve to artificially prolong life and may include mechanical ventilation, dialysis, antibiotics, artificial nutrition and hydration, and other forms of treatment which sustain, restore, or supplant vital bodily functions, but do not include care necessary to provide comfort or to alleviate pain.

(6) "Minor or minor child" means an individual who has not attained the age of 18 years and who has not been emancipated. (1993, c. 150.)

§ 32A-30. Who may make an authorization to consent to health care for minor.

Any custodial parent having understanding and capacity to make and communicate health care decisions who is 18 years of age or older or who is emancipated may make an authorization to consent to health care for the parent's minor child. (1993, c. 150, s. 1.)

§ 32A-31. Extent and limitations of authority.

(a) A custodial parent of a minor child, pursuant to an authorization to consent to health care for minor, may grant an agent full power and authority to consent to and authorize health care for the minor child to the same extent that a custodial parent could give such consent and authorization.

(b) An authorization to consent to health care for minor may contain, and the authority of the agent designated shall be subject to, any specific limitations or restrictions as the custodial parent deems appropriate.

(c) A custodial parent may not, pursuant to an authorization to consent to health care for minor, authorize an agent to consent to the withholding or withdrawal of life sustaining procedures. (1993, c. 150, s. 1.)

§ 32A-32. Duration of authorization; revocation.

(a) An authorization to consent to health care for minor shall be automatically revoked as follows:

(1) If the authorization to consent to health care for minor specifies a date after which it shall not be effective, then the authorization shall be automatically revoked upon such date.

(2) An authorization to consent to health care for minor shall be revoked upon the minor child's attainment of the age of 18 years or upon the minor child's emancipation.

(3) An authorization to consent to health care for minor executed by a custodial parent shall be revoked upon the termination of such custodial parent's rights to custody of the minor child.

(b) An authorization to consent to health care for minor may be revoked at any time by the custodial parent making such authorization. The custodial parent may exercise such right of revocation by executing and acknowledging an instrument of revocation, by executing and acknowledging a subsequent authorization to consent to health care for the minor, or in any other manner in which the custodial parent is able to communicate the parent's intent to revoke.

Such revocation shall become effective only upon communication by the custodial parent to the agent named in the revoked authorization.

(c)   In the event of a disagreement regarding the health care for a minor child between two or more agents authorized pursuant to this Article to consent to and authorize health care for a minor, or between any such agent and a parent of the minor, whether or not the parent is a custodial parent, then any authorization to consent to health care for minor designating any person as an agent shall be revoked during the period of such disagreement, and the provisions of health care for the minor during such period shall be governed by the common law, the provisions of Article 1A of Chapter 90, and other provisions of law, as if no authorization to consent to health care for minor had been executed.

(d)   An authorization to consent to health care for minor shall not be affected by the subsequent incapacity or mental incompetence of the custodial parent making such authorization. (1993, c. 150, s. 1.)

§ 32A-33. Reliance on authorization to consent to health care for minor.

(a)   Any physician, dentist, or other health care provider involved in the health care of a minor child may rely upon the authority of the agent named in a signed and acknowledged authorization to consent to health care for minor in the absence of actual knowledge that the authorization has been revoked or is otherwise invalid.

(b)   Any consent to health care for a minor child given by an agent pursuant to an authorization to consent to health care for minor shall have the same effect as if the custodial parent making the authorization were present and acting on behalf of the parent's minor child. Any physician, dentist, or other health care provider relying in good faith on the authority of an agent shall be protected to the full extent of the power conferred upon the agent, and no person so relying on the authority of the agent shall be liable, by reason of reliance, for actions taken pursuant to a consent of the agent. (1993, c. 150, s. 1.)

§ 32A-34. Statutory form authorization to consent to health care for minor.

The use of the following form in the creation of any authorization to consent to health care for minor is lawful and, when used, it shall meet the requirements and be construed in accordance with the provisions of this Article.

"Authorization to Consent

to Health Care for Minor."

I, _____, of _____ County, _____, am the custodial parent having legal custody of_____, a minor child, age_____, born_____, ____ . I authorize_____, an adult in whose care the minor child has been entrusted, and who resides at_____, to do any acts which may be necessary or proper to provide for the health care of the minor child, including, but not limited to, the power (i) to provide for such health care at any hospital or other institution, or the employing of any physician, dentist, nurse, or other person whose services may be needed for such health care, and (ii) to consent to and authorize any health care, including administration of anesthesia, X-ray examination, performance of operations, and other procedures by physicians, dentists, and other medical personnel except the withholding or withdrawal of life sustaining procedures.

[Optional: This consent shall be effective from the date of execution to and including_____,_____].

By signing here, I indicate that I have the understanding and capacity to communicate health care decisions and that I am fully informed as to the contents of this document and understand the full import of this grant of powers to the agent named herein.

(SEAL)

Custodial Parent   Date

STATE OF NORTH CAROLINA

COUNTY OF

On this _____ day of _____, ____, personally appeared before me the named _____, to me known and known to me to be the person described in and who executed the foregoing instrument and he (or she) acknowledges that he (or she) executed the same and being duly sworn by me, made oath that the statements in the foregoing instrument are true.

Notary Public

My Commission Expires:

(OFFICIAL SEAL). (1993, c. 150, s. 1; 1999-456, s. 59.)

§ 32A-35. Reserved for future codification purposes.

§ 32A-36. Reserved for future codification purposes.

§ 32A-37. Reserved for future codification purposes.

§ 32A-38. Reserved for future codification purposes.

§ 32A-39. Reserved for future codification purposes.

Article 5.

Enforcement of Power of Attorney.

§ 32A-40. Reliance on power of attorney.

(a) Unless (i) a person has actual knowledge that a writing is not a valid power of attorney, or (ii) the action taken or to be taken by a person named as attorney-in-fact in a writing that purports to confer a power of attorney is beyond the apparent power or authority of that named attorney-in-fact as granted in that writing, a person who in good faith relies on a writing that on its face is duly signed, acknowledged, and otherwise appears regular, and that purports to confer a power of attorney, durable or otherwise, shall be protected to the full extent of the powers and authority that reasonably appear to be granted to the attorney-in-fact designated in that writing, and no person so dealing in good faith with that named attorney-in-fact shall be held responsible for any breach of fiduciary duty by that attorney-in-fact, including any breach of loyalty, any act of self-dealing, or any misapplication of money or other property paid or transferred as directed by that attorney-in-fact. This subsection applies without regard to whether or not the person dealing with the attorney-in-fact demands or receives an affidavit under subsection (b) of this section. A person who conducts activities through employees or other agents has actual knowledge of a fact involving a power of attorney only from the time the information was received by an employee or agent having the authority to approve the power of attorney presented.

(b) A person may, prior to acceptance of the authority of the attorney-in-fact or at any other time, request an affidavit executed by the attorney-in-fact to the effect that the attorney-in-fact did not have, at the time of the presentation to the person of the writing purporting to confer a power of attorney, actual knowledge of either (i) the revocation of the power of attorney, or (ii) facts that would cause the attorney-in-fact to question the authenticity or validity of the power of attorney. An affidavit meeting the requirements of this subsection shall be sufficient proof to the requesting person, as of the date of the affidavit, of (i) the nonrevocation of the power of attorney, and (ii) the authenticity and validity of the power of attorney. If the exercise of the power of attorney requires execution and delivery of an instrument that is recordable, the affidavit shall be prepared so as to be recordable. An affidavit prepared under this subsection may also be used as an affidavit under G.S. 32A-13(c). An affidavit in the form described in subsection (d) of this section shall be deemed to meet the requirements of this subsection but shall not be the sole means of meeting those requirements.

(c) This section does not affect any provision in a power of attorney for its termination by expiration of time or occurrence of an event other than an express revocation or a change in the principal's capacity.

(d) Example of Affidavit of Attorney-in-Fact.

STATE OF _____

COUNTY OF _____

The undersigned does hereby state and affirm the following:

(1) The undersigned is the person named as Attorney-in-Fact in the Power of Attorney executed by _____ ("Principal") on [date]_____, _____ (the "Power of Attorney").

(2) The Power of Attorney is currently exercisable by the undersigned.

(3) The undersigned has no actual knowledge of any of the following:

a. The Principal is deceased.

b. The Power of Attorney has been revoked or terminated, partially or otherwise.

c. The Principal lacked the understanding and capacity to make and communicate decisions regarding his estate and person at the time the Power of Attorney was executed.

d. The Power of Attorney was not properly executed and is not a legal, valid power of attorney.

(4) The undersigned agrees not to exercise any powers granted under the Power of Attorney if the undersigned becomes aware that the Principal is deceased or has revoked such powers.

This is the _____ day of _____.

[Signature]

[Acknowledgement]

(2005-178, s. 1.)

§ 32A-41. Penalty for unreasonable refusal to recognize power.

(a) A person dealing with an attorney-in-fact who unreasonably refuses to accept a power of attorney shall be subject to all of the following:

(1) Liability for reasonable attorneys' fees and costs incurred in any action or proceeding necessary to confirm the validity of a power of attorney or to implement a power of attorney.

(2) An order of the court requiring acceptance of the valid power of attorney.

(3) Any other remedy available under applicable law.

(b) Acceptance of a power of attorney shall mean (i) acknowledging the validity and authenticity of the document, and (ii) allowing the attorney-in-fact to conduct business in accordance with the powers that reasonably appear to be granted in the document. (2005-178, s. 1.)

§ 32A-42. Protection for third parties.

(a) A person is not required to honor the attorney-in-fact's authority or to conduct business with the attorney-in-fact if the person is not otherwise required to conduct business with the principal in the same circumstances.

(b) Without limiting the generality of subsection (a) of this section, nothing in this Article requires a person to do any of the following:

(1) Engage in any transaction with an attorney-in-fact if the attorney-in-fact has previously breached any agreement with the person, whether in an individual or fiduciary capacity.

(2) Open an account for a principal at the request of an attorney-in-fact if the principal is not currently a customer of the person.

(3) Make a loan to the principal at the request of the attorney-in-fact.

(c) A person who is presented with a power of attorney shall not be deemed to have unreasonably refused to accept the power of attorney solely on the basis of failure to accept the power of attorney within seven business days.

(d) A person who has reasonable cause to question the authenticity or validity of a power of attorney may refuse to accept the authority granted by that document.

(e) A person who promptly requests, and does not within a reasonable time receive, an affidavit as described in G.S. 32A-40(b), is not deemed under G.S. 32A-41 to have unreasonably refused to accept a power of attorney.

(f) The principal, the attorney-in-fact, or a person presented with a power of attorney may initiate a special proceeding in accordance with the procedures of Article 33 of Chapter 1 of the General Statutes to request a determination of the validity of the power of attorney. If the decision in that special proceeding is that reasonable cause to refuse to accept the power of attorney existed, and that the attorney-in-fact willfully misrepresented the authenticity or validity of the power of attorney, the attorney-in-fact, and not the principal, is liable for reasonable attorneys' fees and costs incurred in that action.

(g) Nothing in this Article requires a person who accepts a power of attorney to permit an attorney-in-fact to conduct business not authorized by the terms of the power of attorney, or otherwise not permitted by applicable statute or regulation.

(h)   Nothing in this Article amends or modifies the rights of banks and other depository institutions to terminate any deposit account in accordance with applicable law. (2005-178, s. 1; 2006-264, s. 39(a).)

§ 32A-43. Scope of Article.

This Article shall apply to all or any portion of a document executed under Article 1, Article 2, or Article 2A of this Chapter. (2005-178, s. 1.)

Chapter 33.

Guardian and Ward.

§§ 33-1 through 33-77: Repealed and recodified.

Chapter 33A.

North Carolina Uniform Transfers to Minors Act

§ 33A-1. Definitions.

In this Chapter:

(1)   "Adult" means an individual who has attained the age of 21 years.

(2)   "Benefit plan" means an employer's plan for the benefit of an employee or partner.

(3)   "Broker" means a person lawfully engaged in the business of effecting transactions in securities or commodities for the person's own account or for the account of others.

(4)   "Court" means the clerk of the superior court of the several counties of the State.

(5) "Custodial property" means (i) any interest in property transferred to a custodian under this Chapter and (ii) the income from and proceeds of that interest in property.

(6) "Custodian" means a person so designated under Section 33A-9 or a successor or substitute custodian designated under Section 33A-18.

(7) "Financial institution" means a bank, trust company, savings and loan associations or other savings institutions, or credit union, chartered and supervised under State or federal law.

(8) "Guardian" means a person appointed or qualified by a court to act as general, limited, or temporary guardian of a minor's property or a person legally authorized to perform substantially the same functions.

(9) "Legal representative" means an individual's personal representative or guardian.

(10) "Member of the minor's family" means the minor's parent, spouse, grandparent, brother, sister, uncle, or aunt, whether of the whole or half blood or by adoption.

(11) "Minor" means an individual who has not attained the age of 21 years.

(12) "Person" means an individual, corporation, organization, or other legal entity.

(13) "Personal representative" means an executor, administrator, successor personal representative, collector, or special administrator of a decedent's estate or a person legally authorized to perform substantially the same function.

(14) "State" includes any state of the United States, the District of Columbia, the Commonwealth of Puerto Rico, and any territory or possession subject to the legislative authority of the United States.

(15) "Transfer" means a transaction that creates custodial property under G.S. 33A-9.

(16) "Transferor" means a person who makes a transfer under this Chapter.

(17) "Trust company" means a financial institution, corporation, or other legal entity, authorized to exercise general trust powers. (1987, c. 563, s. 2.)

§ 33A-2. Scope and jurisdiction.

(a) This Chapter applies to a transfer if at the time of the transfer, the transferor, the minor, or the custodian is a resident of this State or the custodial property is located in this State and the transfer instrument refers to this Chapter in the designation under G.S. 33A-9(a) by which the transfer is made. The custodianship so created remains subject to this Chapter despite a subsequent change in residence of a transferor, the minor, or the custodian, or the removal of custodial property from this State.

(b) A person designated as custodian under this Chapter is subject to personal jurisdiction in this State with respect to any matter relating to the custodianship.

(c) A transfer that purports to be made and which is valid under the Uniform Transfers to Minors Act, the Uniform Gifts to Minors Act, or a substantially similar act, of another state is governed by the law of the designated state and may be executed and is enforceable in this State if at the time of the transfer, the transferor, the minor, or the custodian is a resident of the designated state or the custodial property is located in the designated state.

(d) This Chapter shall not be construed to be the exclusive procedures for transferring property interests to minors and any other procedure for such transfers authorized by the law of this State and, not specifically repealed shall continue in effect. (1987, c. 563, s. 2.)

§ 33A-3. Nomination of custodian.

(a) A person having the right to designate the recipient of property transferable upon the occurrence of a future event may revocably nominate a custodian to receive the property for a minor beneficiary upon the occurrence of the event by naming the custodian followed in substance by the words: "as custodian for _____ (name of minor) under the North Carolina Uniform Transfers to Minors Act." The nomination may name one or more persons as substitute custodians to whom the property must be transferred, in the order named, if the first nominated custodian dies before the transfer or is unable, declines, or is ineligible to serve. The nomination may be made in a will, a trust, a deed, an instrument exercising a power of appointment, or in a writing designating a beneficiary of contractual rights which is registered with or delivered to the payor, issuer, or other obligor of the contractual rights.

(b) A custodian nominated under this section must be a person to whom a transfer of property of that kind may be made under G.S. 33A-9(a).

(c) The nomination of a custodian under this section does not create custodial property until the nominating instrument becomes irrevocable or a transfer to the nominated custodian is completed under G.S. 33A-9. Unless the nomination of a custodian has been revoked, upon the occurrence of the future event the custodianship becomes effective and the custodian shall enforce a transfer of the custodial property pursuant to G.S. 33A-9. (1987, c. 563, s. 2.)

§ 33A-4. Transfer by gift or exercise of power of appointment.

A person may make a transfer by irrevocable gift to, or the irrevocable exercise of a power of appointment in favor of, a custodian for the benefit of a minor pursuant to G.S. 33A-9. (1987, c. 563, s. 2.)

§ 33A-5. Transfer authorized by will or trust.

(a) A personal representative or trustee may make an irrevocable transfer pursuant to G.S. 33A-9 to a custodian for the benefit of a minor as authorized in the governing will or trust.

(b) If the testator or settlor has nominated a custodian under G.S. 33A-3 to receive the custodial property, the transfer must be made to that person.

(c) If the testator or settlor has not nominated a custodian under G.S. 33A-3, or all persons so nominated as custodian die before the transfer or are unable, decline, or are ineligible to serve the personal representative or the trustee, as the case may be, shall designate the custodian from among those eligible to serve as custodian for property of that kind under G.S. 33A-9(a). (1987, c. 563, s. 2.)

§ 33A-6. Other transfer by fiduciary.

(a)   Subject to subsection (c), a personal representative or trustee may make an irrevocable transfer to the transferor or to another adult or trust company as custodian for the benefit of a minor pursuant to G.S. 33A-9, in the absence of a will or under a will or trust that does not contain an authorization to do so.

(b)   Subject to subsection (c), a guardian may make an irrevocable transfer to the transferor or to another adult or trust company as custodian for the benefit of the minor pursuant to Section 33A-9.

(c)   A transfer under subsection (a) or (b) may be made only if (i) the personal representative, trustee, or guardian considers the transfer to be in the best interest of the minor, and (ii) the transfer is not prohibited by or inconsistent with provisions of the applicable will, trust agreement, or other governing instrument. If the value of the property transferred under subsections (a) or (b) will total more than ten thousand dollars ($10,000), whether in one or more transfers, that transfer must be authorized by the court. If a transfer under subsections (a) or (b) is to the transferor then the transfer must be authorized by the court. (1987, c. 563, s. 2.)

§ 33A-7. Transfer by obligor.

(a)   Subject to subsections (b) and (c), a person not subject to Section 33A-5 or 33A-6 who holds property of or owes a liquidated debt to a minor not having a guardian may make an irrevocable transfer to a custodian for the benefit of the minor pursuant to Section 33A-9.

(b)   If a person having the right to do so under Section 33A-3 has nominated a custodian under that section to receive the custodial property, the transfer must be made to that person.

(c)   If no custodian has been nominated under Section 33A-3, or all persons so nominated as custodian die before the transfer or are unable, decline, or are ineligible to serve, a transfer under this section may be made to an adult member of the minor's family or to a trust company if the aggregate value of the property does not exceed ten thousand dollars ($10,000) in value. (1987, c. 563, s. 2.)

§ 33A-8. Receipt for custodial property.

A written acknowledgement by a custodian of delivery authorized by this Chapter constitutes a sufficient receipt and discharge for custodial property transferred to the custodian. (1987, c. 563, s. 2.)

§ 33A-9. Manner of creating custodial property and effecting transfer; designation of initial custodian; control.

(a)   Custodial property is created and a transfer is made whenever:

(1)   An uncertificated security or a certificated security in registered form is either:

a.   Registered in the name of the transferor, an adult other than the transferor, or a trust company, followed in substance by the words: "as custodian for _____ (name of minor) under the North Carolina Uniform Transfers to Minors Act"; or

b.   Delivered if in certificated form, or any document necessary for the transfer of an uncertificated security is delivered, together with any necessary endorsement to an adult other than the transferor or to a trust company as custodian, accompanied by an instrument in substantially the form set forth in subsection (b);

(2)   Money is paid or delivered, or a security held in the name of a broker, financial institution, or its nominee is transferred, to a broker or financial institution for credit to an account in the name of the transferor, an adult other than the transferor, or a trust company, followed in substance by the words: "as

custodian for _____ (name of minor) under the North Carolina Uniform Transfers to Minors Act";

(3)　　The ownership of a life or endowment insurance policy or annuity contract is either:

a.　　Registered with the issuer in the name of the transferor, an adult other than the transferor, or a trust company, followed in substance by the words: "as custodian for _____ (name of minor) under the North Carolina Uniform Transfers to Minors Act"; or

b.　　Assigned in a writing delivered to an adult other than the transferor or to a trust company whose name in the assignment is followed in substance by the words: "as custodian for _____ (name of minor) under the North Carolina Uniform Transfers to Minors Act";

(4)　　An irrevocable exercise of a power of appointment or an irrevocable present right to future payment under a contract is the subject of a written notification delivered to the payor, issuer, or other obligor that the right is transferred to the transferor, an adult other than the transferor, or a trust company, whose name in the notification is followed in substance by the words: "as custodian for _____ (name of minor) under the North Carolina Uniform Transfers to Minors Act";

(5)　　An interest in real property is conveyed or devised to the transferor, an adult other than the transferor, or a trust company, whose name in the conveyance is followed in substance by the words: "as custodian for _____ (name of minor) under the North Carolina Uniform Transfers to Minors Act";

(6)　　A certificate of title issued by a department or agency of a state or of the United States which evidences title to tangible personal property is either:

a.　　Issued in the name of the transferor, an adult other than the transferor, or a trust company, followed in substance by the words: "as custodian for _____ (name of minor) under the North Carolina Uniform Transfers to Minors Act"; or

b.　　Delivered to an adult other than the transferor or to a trust company, endorsed to that person followed in substance by the words: "as custodian for

_____ (name of minor) under the North Carolina Uniform Transfers to Minors Act"; or

(7) An interest in any property not described in paragraphs (1) through (6) is transferred to an adult other than the transferor or to a trust company by a written instrument in substantially the form set forth in subsection (b).

(b) An instrument in the following form satisfies the requirements of paragraphs (1)b. and (7) of subsection (a):

TRANSFER UNDER THE NORTH CAROLINA

UNIFORM TRANSFERS TO MINORS ACT

I, _____ (name of transferor or name and representative capacity if a fiduciary) hereby transfer to _____ (name of custodian), as custodian for _____ (name of minor) under the North Carolina Uniform Transfers to Minors Act, the following: (insert a description of the custodial property sufficient to identify it).

Dated: _____

_____

(Signature)

_____ (name of custodian) acknowledges receipt of the property described above as custodian for the minor named above under the North Carolina Uniform Transfers to Minors Act.

Dated: _____

_____

(Signature of Custodian)

(c) A transferor shall place the custodian in control of the custodial property as soon as practicable. (1987, c. 563, s. 2; 1997-456, s. 27.)

§ 33A-10. Single custodianship.

A transfer may be made only for one minor, and only one person may be the custodian. All custodial property held under this Chapter by the same custodian for the benefit of the same minor constitutes a single custodianship. (1987, c. 563, s. 2.)

§ 33A-11. Validity and effect of transfer.

(a) The validity of a transfer made in a manner prescribed in this Chapter is not affected by:

(1) Failure of the transferor to comply with G.S. 33A-9(c) concerning control;

(2) Designation of an ineligible custodian, except designation of the transferor in the case of property for which the transferor is ineligible to serve as custodian under G.S. 33A-9(a);

(3) Death or incapacity of a person nominated under G.S. 33A-3 or designated under G.S. 33A-9 as custodian or the disclaimer of the office by that person; or

(4) The use of an abbreviation in referring to this Chapter or the equivalent act of another state.

(b) A transfer made pursuant to G.S. 33A-9 is irrevocable, and the custodial property is indefeasibly vested in the minor, but the custodian has all the rights, powers, duties, and authority provided in this Chapter, and neither the minor nor the minor's legal representative has any right, power, duty, or authority with respect to the custodial property except as provided in this Chapter.

(c) By making a transfer, the transferor incorporates in the disposition all the provisions of this Chapter and grants to the custodian, and to any third person dealing with a person designated as custodian, the respective powers, rights, and immunities provided in this Chapter. (1987, c. 563, s. 2.)

§ 33A-12. Care of custodial property.

(a) A custodian shall:

(1) Take control of custodial property;

(2) Register or record title to custodial property if appropriate; and

(3) Collect, hold, manage, invest, and reinvest custodial property.

(b) In dealing with custodial property, a custodian shall observe the standard of care that would be observed by a prudent person dealing with property of another and is not limited by any other statute restricting investments by fiduciaries. If a custodian has a special skill or expertise or is named custodian on the basis of representations of a special skill or expertise, the custodian shall use that skill or expertise. However, a custodian, in the custodian's discretion and without liability to the minor or the minor's estate, may retain any custodial property received from a transferor.

(c) A custodian may invest in or pay premiums on life insurance or endowment policies on (i) the life of the minor only if the minor or the minor's estate or the custodian in the capacity of custodian is the sole beneficiary, or (ii) the life of another person in whom the minor has an insurable interest only to the extent that the minor, the minor's estate, or the custodian in the capacity of custodian, is the irrevocable beneficiary.

(d) A custodian at all times shall keep custodial property separate and distinct from all other property in a manner sufficient to identify it clearly as custodial property of the minor. Custodial property may be held with other owners if owned as tenants in common, provided that the property interest of the owners is fixed. Custodial property subject to recordation is so identified if it is recorded, and custodial property subject to registration is so identified if it is either registered, or held in an account designated, in the name of the custodian, followed in substance by the words: "as a custodian for

_____ (name of minor) under the North Carolina Uniform Transfers to Minors Act."

(e) A custodian shall keep records of all transactions with respect to custodial property, including information necessary for the preparation of the minor's tax returns, and shall make them available for inspection at reasonable intervals by a parent or legal representative of the minor, or by the minor if the minor has attained the age of 14 years. (1987, c. 563, s. 2.)

§ 33A-13. Powers of custodian.

(a) A custodian, acting in a custodial capacity, has all the rights, powers, and authority over custodial property that unmarried adult owners have over their own property, but a custodian may exercise those rights, powers, and authority in the capacity of a custodian only.

(b) This section does not relieve a custodian from liability for breach of G.S. 33A-12. (1987, c. 563, s. 2.)

§ 33A-14. Use of custodial property.

(a) A custodian may deliver or pay to the minor or expend for the minor's benefit so much of the custodial property as the custodian considers advisable for the use and benefit of the minor, without court order and without regard to (i) the duty or ability of the custodian personally or of any other person to support the minor, or (ii) any other income or property of the minor which may be applicable or available for that purpose.

(b) On petition of an interested person or the minor if the minor has attained the age of 14 years, the court may order the custodian to deliver or pay to the minor or expend for the minor's benefit so much of the custodial property as the court considers advisable for the use and benefit of the minor.

(c) A delivery, payment, or expenditure under this section is in addition to, not in substitution for, and does not affect any obligation of a person to support the minor. (1987, c. 563, s. 2.)

§ 33A-15. Custodian's expenses, compensation, and bond.

(a)   A custodian is entitled to pay from and to be reimbursed from custodial property for reasonable expenses incurred in the performance of the custodian's duties.

(b)   Except for one who is a transferor under G.S. 33A-4, a custodian has a noncumulative election during each calendar year to charge reasonable compensation for services performed during that year.

(c)   Except as provided in G.S. 33A-18(f), a custodian need not give a bond. (1987, c. 563, s. 2.)

§ 33A-16. Exemption of third person from liability.

A third person in good faith and without court order may act on the instructions of or otherwise deal with any person purporting to make a transfer or purporting to act in the capacity of a custodian and, in the absence of knowledge, is not responsible for determining:

(1)   The validity of the purported custodian's designation;

(2)   The propriety of, or the authority under this Chapter for, any act of the purported custodian;

(3)   The validity or propriety under this Chapter of any instrument or instructions executed or given either by the person purporting to make a transfer or by the purported custodian; or

(4)   The propriety of the application of any property of the minor delivered to the purported custodian. (1987, c. 563, s. 2.)

§ 33A-17. Liability to third persons.

(a) A claim based on (i) a contract entered into by a custodian acting in a custodial capacity, (ii) an obligation arising from the ownership or control of custodial property, or (iii) a tort committed during the custodianship, may be asserted against the custodial property by proceeding against the custodian in the custodial capacity, whether or not the custodian or the minor is personally liable therefor.

(b) A custodian may be held personally liable:

(1) On a contract properly entered into in the custodial capacity if the custodian fails to reveal that capacity and to identify the custodianship in the contract; or

(2) For an obligation arising from control of custodial property or for a tort committed during the custodianship if the custodian is personally at fault.

(c) A minor is not personally liable for an obligation arising from ownership of custodial property or for a tort committed during the custodianship unless the minor is personally at fault. (1987, c. 563, s. 2.)

§ 33A-18. Renunciation, resignation, death, or removal of custodian; designation of successor custodian.

(a) A person nominated under G.S. 33A-3 or designated under G.S. 33A-9 as custodian may decline to serve by delivering a written disclaimer to the person who made the nomination or to the transferor or the transferor's legal representative. If the event giving rise to a transfer has not occurred and no substitute custodian able, willing, and eligible to serve was nominated under G.S. 33A-3, the person who made the nomination may nominate a substitute custodian under G.S. 33A-3; otherwise the transferor or the transferor's legal representative shall designate a substitute custodian at the time of the transfer, in either case from among the persons eligible to serve as custodian for that kind of property under G.S. 33A-9(a).

(b) A custodian at any time may designate a trust company or an adult other than the transferor under G.S. 33A-4 as successor custodian by executing and dating an instrument of designation before a subscribing witness other than the successor. If the instrument of designation does not contain or is not accompanied by the resignation of the custodian, the designation of the successor does not take effect until the custodian resigns, dies, becomes incapacitated, or is removed.

(c)   A custodian may resign at any time by delivering written notice to the minor if the minor has attained the age of 14 years and to the successor custodian and by delivering the custodial property to the successor custodian.

(d)   If a custodian is ineligible, dies, or becomes incapacitated without having effectively designated a successor and the minor has attained the age of 14 years, the minor may designate as successor custodian, in the manner prescribed in subsection (b), an adult member of the minor's family, a guardian of the minor, or a trust company. If the minor has not attained the age of 14 years or fails to act within 60 days after the ineligibility, death, or incapacity, the guardian of the minor becomes successor custodian. If the minor has no guardian or the guardian declines to act, the transferor, the legal representative of the transferor or of the custodian, an adult member of the minor's family, or any other interested person may petition the court to designate a successor custodian.

(e)   A custodian who declines to serve under subsection (a) or resigns under subsection (c), or the legal representative of a deceased or incapacitated custodian, as soon as practicable, shall put the custodial property and records in the possession and control of the successor custodian. The successor custodian by action may enforce the obligation to deliver custodial property and records and becomes responsible for each item as received.

(f)   A transferor, the legal representative of a transferor, an adult member of the minor's family, a guardian of the person of the minor, the guardian of the minor, or the minor if the minor has attained the age of 14 years may petition the court to remove the custodian for cause and to designate a successor custodian other than a transferor under G.S. 33A-4 or to require the custodian to give appropriate bond. (1987, c. 563, s. 2.)

§ 33A-19. Accounting by and determination of liability of custodian.

(a)   A minor who has attained the age of 14 years, the minor's guardian of the person or legal representative, an adult member of the minor's family, a transferor, or a transferor's legal representative may petition the court (i) for an accounting by the custodian or the custodian's legal representative; or (ii) for a determination of responsibility, as between the custodial property and the custodian personally, for claims against the custodial property unless the responsibility has been adjudicated in an action under G.S. 33A-17 to which the minor or the minor's legal representative was a party.

(b) A successor custodian may petition the court for an accounting by the predecessor custodian.

(c) The court, in a proceeding under this Chapter or the presiding judge in any other proceeding, may require or permit the custodian or the custodian's legal representative to account.

(d) If a custodian is removed under G.S. 33A-18(f), the court shall require an accounting and order delivery of the custodial property and records to the successor custodian and the execution of all instruments required for transfer of the custodial property. (1987, c. 563, s. 2.)

§ 33A-20. Termination of custodianship.

The custodian shall transfer in an appropriate manner the custodial property to the minor or to the minor's estate upon the earlier of:

(1) The minor's attainment of 21 years of age with respect to custodial property transferred under G.S. 33A-4 or G.S. 33A-5, except that any transferor may have custodial property transferred to the minor at any time after the age of 18 and before the age of 21 by a designation in the following words or their equivalent: "The custodian shall transfer this property to _____ (name of minor) when he reaches the age of ___ (age after 18 and before 21).";

(2) The minor's attainment of age 18 with respect to custodial property transferred under G.S. 33A-6 or G.S. 33A-7; or

(3) The minor's death. (1987, c. 563, s. 2.)

§ 33A-21. Applicability.

This Chapter applies to a transfer within the scope of G.S. 33A-2 made after October 1, 1987, if:

(1) The transfer purports to have been made under the Uniform Gifts to Minors Act of North Carolina; or

(2) The instrument by which the transfer purports to have been made uses in substance the designation "as custodian under the Uniform Gifts to Minors Act" or "as custodian under the Uniform Transfers to Minors Act" of any other state, and the application of this Chapter is necessary to validate the transfer. (1987, c. 563, s. 2.)

§ 33A-22. Effect on existing custodianships.

(a) Any transfer of custodial property as now defined in this Chapter made before October 1, 1987, is validated notwithstanding that there was no specific authority in the Uniform Gifts to Minors Act of North Carolina for the coverage of custodial property of that kind or for a transfer from that source at the time the transfer was made.

(b) This Chapter applies to all transfers made before October 1, 1987, in a manner and form prescribed in the Uniform Gifts to Minors Act of North Carolina, except insofar as the application impairs constitutionally vested rights or extends the duration of custodianships in existence on October 1, 1987.

(c) G.S. 33A-1 and G.S. 33A-20 with respect to the age of a minor for whom custodial property is held under this Chapter shall not apply to custodial property held in a custodianship that terminated because of the minor's attainment of the age of majority and before October 1, 1987. (1987, c. 563, s. 2.)

§ 33A-23. Uniformity of application and construction.

This Chapter shall be applied and construed to effect its general purpose to make uniform the law with respect to the subject of this Chapter among states enacting it. (1987, c. 563, s. 2.)

§ 33A-24. Short title.

This Chapter may be cited as the "North Carolina Uniform Transfers to Minors Act." (1987, c. 563, s. 2.)

Chapter 33B.

North Carolina Uniform Custodial Trust Act.

§ 33B-1. Definitions.

As used in this act:

(1)   "Adult" means an individual who is at least 21 years of age.

(2)   "Beneficiary" means an individual for whom property has been transferred to or held under a declaration of trust by a custodial trustee for the individual's use and benefit under this act.

(3)   "Guardian of the estate" means a guardian appointed for the purpose of managing the property, estate, and business affairs of a ward, or a person legally authorized to perform substantially the same functions. As used in this act the term "guardian of the estate" includes a general guardian or guardian of the estate appointed under the provisions of Chapter 35A of the General Statutes.

(4)   "Court" means the clerk of superior court of this State.

(5)   "Custodial trust property" means an interest in property transferred to or held under a declaration of trust by a custodial trustee under this act and the income from and proceeds of that interest.

(6)   "Custodial trustee" means a person designated as trustee of a custodial trust under this act or a substitute or successor to the person designated.

(7)   "Guardian of the person" means a guardian appointed for the purpose of performing duties relating to the care, custody, and control of a ward, but not a person who is only a guardian ad litem. As used in this act the term "guardian of the person" includes a general guardian or guardian of the person appointed under the provisions of Chapter 35A of the General Statutes.

(8) "Incapacitated" means lacking the ability to manage property and business affairs effectively by reason of mental illness, mental deficiency, physical illness or disability, chronic use of drugs, chronic intoxication, confinement, detention by a foreign power, disappearance, being under 21 years of age, or other disabling cause.

(9) "Legal representative" means a personal representative or guardian of the estate.

(10) "Member of the beneficiary's family" means a beneficiary's spouse, descendant, parent, grandparent, brother, sister, uncle or aunt, whether of the whole or half blood or by adoption.

(11) "Person" means an individual, corporation, business trust, estate, trust, partnership, joint venture, association, or any other legal or commercial entity.

(12) "Personal representative" means an executor, administrator, or special administrator of a decedent's estate, a person legally authorized to perform substantially the same function, or a successor to any of them.

(13) "State" means a state, territory, or possession of the United States, the District of Columbia, or the Commonwealth of Puerto Rico.

(14) "Transferor" means a person who creates a custodial trust by transfer or declaration.

(15) "Trust company" means a financial institution, corporation, or other legal entity, authorized to exercise general trust powers in North Carolina.

(16) "General guardian" means a guardian of both the estate and the person. (1995, c. 486, s. 1.)

§ 33B-2. Custodial trust; general.

(a) A person may create a custodial trust of property by a written transfer of the property to a trust company or an adult other than the transferor executed in any lawful manner, naming as beneficiary an individual, who may be the transferor, in which the transferee is designated, in substance, as custodial trustee under the North Carolina Uniform Custodial Trust Act. A transfer is executed in a lawful manner if the formalities, if any, of the transfer of the particular property necessary under general principles of law are satisfied.

(b)   An adult may create a custodial trust of property by a written declaration which names as beneficiary an individual other than the declarant. The declaration shall be evidenced by registration of the property or by other instrument of declaration executed in any lawful manner, describing the property and designating the declarant, in substance, as custodial trustee under the North Carolina Uniform Custodial Trust Act. A registration or other declaration of trust for the sole benefit of the declarant is not a custodial trust under this act. A registration or declaration is executed in a lawful manner if the formalities, if any, of the transfer of the beneficial interest in the particular property under general principles of law are satisfied.

(c)   Title to custodial trust property is in the custodial trustee, and the beneficial interest is in the beneficiary.

(d)   Except as provided in subsection (e) of this section, a transferor may not terminate a custodial trust.

(e)   The beneficiary, if not incapacitated, or the guardian of the estate of an incapacitated beneficiary, may terminate a custodial trust by delivering to the custodial trustee a writing signed by the beneficiary or guardian of the estate declaring the termination. If not previously terminated, the custodial trust terminates on the death of the beneficiary.

(f)   Any person may augment existing custodial trust property by the addition of other property pursuant to a written instrument satisfying the requirements of subsections (a) or (b) of this section.

(g)   The transferor may designate, or authorize the designation of, a successor custodial trustee in the trust instrument.

(h)   This act does not displace or restrict other means of creating trusts. A trust, the terms of which do not conform to this act, may be enforceable according to its terms under the law. (1995, c. 486, s. 1.)

§ 33B-3. Custodial trust to begin in the future.

(a) A person may create a custodial trust to begin in the future by designating the transferee in substance "as custodial trustee for _____ (name of beneficiary) under the North Carolina Uniform Custodial Trust Act". A designation under this section may be made in:

(1) A will;

(2) A trust;

(3) An insurance policy;

(4) A deed;

(5) A payable-on-death account;

(6) An instrument exercising a power of appointment, provided that the donor of the power has not expressly prohibited the exercise of the power in favor of a custodial trustee, and provided further that the beneficiary of the custodial trust is a permissible object of the power, although the custodial trustee need not be a permissible object of the power; or

(7) A writing designating a beneficiary of contractual rights, including but not limited to rights under a pension or profit sharing plan, which is registered with or delivered to the fiduciary, payor, issuer, or obligor of the contractual right.

(b) Persons may be designated as substitute or successor custodial trustees to whom the property must be paid or transferred in the order named if the preceding designated custodial trustee is unable or unwilling to serve. (1995, c. 486, s. 1.)

§ 33B-4. Form and effect of receipt and acceptance by custodial trustee; jurisdiction.

(a) Obligations of a custodial trustee, including the obligation to follow directions of the beneficiary, arise under this act upon the custodial trustee's acceptance, express or implied, of the custodial trust property.

(b) The custodial trustee's acceptance may be evidenced by a writing stating in substance:

"CUSTODIAL TRUSTEE'S RECEIPT AND ACCEPTANCE

I, _____, (name of custodial trustee) acknowledge receipt of the custodial trust property described below or in the attached instrument and accept the custodial trust as custodial trustee for _____ (name of beneficiary) under the North Carolina Uniform Custodial Trust Act. I undertake to administer and distribute the custodial trust property pursuant to the North Carolina Uniform Custodial Trust Act. My obligations as custodial trustee are subject to the directions of the beneficiary unless the beneficiary is designated as, is, or becomes incapacitated. The custodial trust property consists of _____

Dated: _____

_____

(Signature of Custodial Trustee)".

(c) Upon accepting custodial trust property, a person designated as custodial trustee under this act is subject to personal jurisdiction in this State with respect to any matter relating to the custodial trust. (1995, c. 486, s. 1.)

§ 33B-5. Transfer to custodial trustee by fiduciary or obligor; facility of payment.

(a) A person, including a fiduciary other than a custodial trustee, who holds property of or owes a debt to an incapacitated individual not having a guardian of the estate may make a transfer to an adult member of the beneficiary's family or to a trust company as custodial trustee for the use and benefit of the incapacitated individual. If the value of the property or the debt exceeds twenty thousand dollars ($20,000), the transfer is not effective unless authorized by the court.

(b) A written acknowledgment of delivery, signed by a custodial trustee, is a sufficient receipt and discharge for property transferred to the custodial trustee pursuant to this section.

(c) This section shall not apply when the disposition of the property has been directed by an instrument designating a custodial trustee pursuant to G.S. 33B-3. (1995, c. 486, s. 1.)

§ 33B-6. Single beneficiaries; separate custodial trusts.

(a) Beneficial interests in a custodial trust may not be created for multiple beneficiaries.

(b) All custodial trust property held under this act by the same custodial trustee for the use and benefit of a single beneficiary may be administered as a single custodial trust. (1995, c. 486, s. 1.)

§ 33B-7. General duties of custodial trustee.

(a) If appropriate, a custodial trustee shall register or record the instrument vesting title to custodial trust property.

(b) If the beneficiary is not incapacitated, a custodial trustee shall follow the directions of the beneficiary in the management, control, investment, or retention of the custodial trust property.

If the beneficiary is incapacitated or the beneficiary has capacity but has not given direction, the custodial trustee shall observe the standard of care that would be observed by a prudent person dealing with property of another and is not limited by any other law restricting investments by fiduciaries. However, a custodial trustee, in the custodial trustee's discretion, may retain any custodial trust property received from the transferor.

If a custodial trustee has a special skill or expertise or is named custodial trustee on the basis of representation of a special skill or expertise, the custodial trustee shall observe the standard of care expected of one with that skill or expertise.

(c) Subject to subsection (b) of this section, a custodial trustee shall take control of and collect, hold, manage, invest, and reinvest custodial trust property.

(d) A custodial trustee at all times shall keep custodial trust property of which the custodial trustee has control, separate from all other property in a manner sufficient to identify it clearly as custodial trust property of the beneficiary. Custodial trust property, the title to which is subject to recordation, is adequately identified as such if an appropriate instrument so identifying the property is recorded in the name of the custodial trustee, designated in substance "as custodial trustee for _____ (name of beneficiary) under the North Carolina Uniform Custodial Trust Act". Custodial trust property subject to registration is so identified if it is registered, or held in an account in the name of the custodial trustee, designated in substance "as custodial trustee for _____ (name of beneficiary) under the North Carolina Uniform Custodial Trust Act".

(e) A custodial trustee shall keep records of all transactions with respect to custodial trust property, including information necessary for the preparation of tax returns, and shall make the records and information available at reasonable times to the beneficiary or legal representative of the beneficiary.

(f) Unless the durable power of attorney specifically provides otherwise, the exercise of the durable power of attorney for an incapacitated beneficiary is not effective to terminate or direct the administration or distribution of a custodial trust. (1995, c. 486, s. 1.)

§ 33B-8. General powers of custodial trustee.

(a) A custodial trustee, acting in a fiduciary capacity, has all the rights and powers over custodial trust property which an unmarried adult owner has over individually owned property, but a custodial trustee may exercise those rights and powers in a fiduciary capacity only.

(b) This section does not relieve a custodial trustee from liability for a violation of G.S. 33B-7. (1995, c. 486, s. 1.)

§ 33B-9. Use of custodial trust property.

(a)   A custodial trustee shall pay to the beneficiary or expend for the beneficiary's use and benefit so much or all of the custodial trust property as the beneficiary while not incapacitated may direct from time to time.

(b)   If the beneficiary is incapacitated, the custodial trustee shall expend so much or all of the custodial trust property as the custodial trustee considers advisable for the use and benefit of the beneficiary and the spouse and children, and other dependents of the beneficiary. Expenditures may be made in the manner, when, and to the extent that the custodial trustee determines suitable and proper, without court order and without regard to other support, income, or property of the beneficiary.

(c)   A custodial trustee may establish checking, savings, or other similar accounts of reasonable amounts from which either the custodial trustee or the beneficiary may withdraw funds or against which either may draw checks. Funds withdrawn from, or checks written against, the account of the beneficiary are distributions of custodial trust property by the custodial trustee to the beneficiary. (1995, c. 486, s. 1.)

§ 33B-10. Determination of incapacity; effect.

(a)   The custodial trustee shall administer the custodial trust as for an incapacitated beneficiary if (i) the custodial trust was created under G.S. 33B-5, (ii) the transferor has so directed in the instrument creating the custodial trust, (iii) a determination that a beneficiary is an incompetent adult has been made under the provisions of Chapter 35A, including a determination of limited incompetence under the provisions of G.S. 35A-1112(d), unless the court provided otherwise, or (iv) the custodial trustee has determined that the beneficiary is incapacitated under subsection (b) of this section.

(b)   A custodial trustee may determine that the beneficiary is incapacitated in reliance upon (i) previous direction or authority given by the beneficiary while not incapacitated, including direction or authority pursuant to a durable power of attorney, (ii) the certificate of the beneficiary's physician, (iii) authority given to the custodial trustee in the instrument creating the trust to determine the incapacity of the beneficiary after the creation of the custodial trust, or (iv) other reasonable evidence.

(c) If a custodial trustee for an incapacitated beneficiary determines that the beneficiary's incapacity has ceased, or that circumstances concerning the beneficiary's ability to manage property and business affairs have changed since the creation of a custodial trust directing administration as for an incapacitated beneficiary, the custodial trustee may administer the trust as for a beneficiary who is not incapacitated.

(d) Regardless of whether any determination of incapacity under subsection (b) of this section has or has not been made, the beneficiary, the custodial trustee, or other person interested in the custodial trust property or the welfare of the beneficiary, may petition under the procedures of Chapter 35A for a determination by the court whether the beneficiary is or continues to be incapacitated as defined in G.S. 33B-1(8). A determination of incapacity does not require appointment of a guardian of the estate unless in the discretion of the court such appointment is otherwise warranted.

(e) Incapacity of a beneficiary does not terminate (i) the custodial trust, (ii) any designation of a successor custodial trustee, (iii) rights or powers of the custodial trustee, or (iv) any immunities of third persons acting on instructions of the custodial trustee.

(f) A custodial trustee shall not be liable for any determinations authorized by this section regarding the capacity or incapacity of the beneficiary made in good faith. (1995, c. 486, s. 1.)

§ 33B-11. Third-party transactions.

A third person in good faith and without a court order may act on instructions of, or otherwise deal with, a person purporting to make a transfer as, or to act in the capacity of, a custodial trustee. In the absence of actual knowledge to the contrary, the third person is not responsible for determining:

(1) The validity of the purported custodial trustee's designation;

(2) The propriety of, or the authority under this act for, any action of the purported custodial trustee;

(3) The validity or propriety of an instrument executed or instruction given pursuant to this act either by the person purporting to make a transfer or declaration or by the purported custodial trustee; or

(4) The propriety of the application of property vested in the purported custodial trustee. (1995, c. 486, s. 1.)

§ 33B-12. Liability to the third person.

(a) A claim based on (i) a contract entered into by a custodial trustee acting in a fiduciary capacity, (ii) an obligation arising from the ownership or control of custodial trust property, (iii) a tort committed in the course of administering the custodial trust, may be asserted by a third person against the custodial trust property by proceeding against the custodial trustee in a fiduciary capacity, whether or not the custodial trustee or the beneficiary is personally liable.

(b) A custodial trustee may be held personally liable to a third person:

(1) On a contract entered into in a fiduciary capacity if the custodial trustee fails to reveal that capacity or to identify the custodial trust in the contract; or

(2) For an obligation arising from control of custodial trust property or for a tort committed in the course of the administration of the custodial trust if the custodial trustee is personally at fault.

(c) A beneficiary is not personally liable to a third person for an obligation arising from beneficial ownership of custodial trust property or for a tort committed in the course of administration of the custodial trust unless the beneficiary is personally in possession of the custodial trust property giving rise to the liability or is personally at fault.

(d) Subsections (b) and (c) of this section do not preclude actions or proceedings to establish liability of the custodial trustee or beneficiary as owner or possessor of the custodial trust property to the extent that person is protected as the insured by liability insurance. (1995, c. 486, s. 1.)

§ 33B-13. Declination, resignation, incapacity, death, or removal of custodial trustee; designation of successor custodial trustee.

(a) Before accepting the custodial trust property, a person designated as custodial trustee may decline to serve by notifying the person who made the designation, the transferor, or the transferor's legal representative. In such case, the transferor or the transferor's legal representative may designate a substitute custodial trustee. If the custodial trust is being created under G.S. 33B-3, the substitute custodial trustee designated under G.S. 33B-3 becomes the custodial trustee, or, if a substitute custodial trustee has not been designated, the person who made the designation may designate a substitute custodial trustee pursuant to G.S. 33B-3.

(b) A custodial trustee who has accepted the custodial trust property may resign by (i) delivering written notice to a successor custodial trustee, if any, the beneficiary, and, if the beneficiary is incapacitated, to the beneficiary's guardian of the estate, if any, and (ii) transferring and, where appropriate, registering or recording an instrument relating to the custodial trust property in the name of the successor custodial trustee identified under subsection (c) of this section.

(c) If a custodial trustee or successor custodial trustee is ineligible, resigns, dies, or becomes incapacitated, the successor designated under G.S. 33B-2 or G.S. 33B-3 becomes custodial trustee. If there is no effective provision for a successor, the beneficiary, if not incapacitated, may designate a successor custodial trustee; if the beneficiary fails to act within 90 days, the resigning custodial trustee may designate a successor custodial trustee. If there is no effective provision for a successor custodial trustee and if the beneficiary is incapacitated, the beneficiary's guardian of the estate becomes successor custodial trustee. If the beneficiary does not have a guardian of the estate or the guardian of the estate fails to act as custodial trustee, the resigning custodial trustee may designate a successor custodial trustee.

(d) If a successor custodial trustee is not designated pursuant to subsection (c) of this section, the following persons may in the order listed petition the court to designate a successor custodial trustee: the transferor, the legal representative of the transferor, the legal representative of the custodial trustee, the general guardian of the beneficiary, the guardian of the estate of the beneficiary, an adult member of the beneficiary's family, a person interested in the custodial trust property, or a person interested in the welfare of the beneficiary.

(e) A custodial trustee who declines to serve or resigns, or the legal representative of a deceased or incapacitated custodial trustee shall put the custodial trust property and records in the possession and control of the successor custodial trustee as soon as practical. The successor custodial trustee shall enforce the obligation to deliver custodial trust property and records.

(f) A beneficiary, the beneficiary's guardian of the estate, an adult member of the beneficiary's family, a guardian of the person of the beneficiary, a person interested in the custodial trust property, or a person interested in the welfare of the beneficiary, may petition the court (i) to remove the custodial trustee for cause and to designate a successor custodial trustee, (ii) to require the custodial trustee to furnish a bond or other security for the faithful performance of fiduciary duties, or (iii) for other appropriate relief. (1995, c. 486, s. 1.)

§ 33B-14. Expenses, compensation, and bond of custodial trustee.

Except as otherwise provided in the instrument creating the custodial trust, in an agreement with the beneficiary, or by court order, a custodial trustee:

(1) Is entitled to reimbursement from custodial trust property for reasonable expenses incurred in the performance of fiduciary services;

(2) May charge, no later than six months after the end of each calendar year, a reasonable compensation for fiduciary services performed during that year; and

(3) Need not furnish a bond or other security for the faithful performance of fiduciary duties. (1995, c. 486, s. 1.)

§ 33B-15. Reporting and accounting by custodial trustee; determination of liability of custodial trustee.

(a) Upon the acceptance of custodial trust property, the custodial trustee shall provide a written statement that the custodial trust property is held pursuant to this act and describing the custodial trust property. The custodial trustee shall thereafter provide a written statement of the administration of the custodial trust property (i) once each year, (ii) upon request at reasonable times by the beneficiary or the beneficiary's legal representative, (iii) upon resignation or removal of the custodial trustee, and (iv) upon termination of the custodial trust. The statements must be provided to the beneficiary or to the beneficiary's legal representative. Upon termination of the beneficiary's interest, the custodial trustee shall furnish a statement to the person to whom the custodial trust property is to be delivered.

(b)   A beneficiary, the beneficiary's legal representative, an adult member of the beneficiary's family, a person interested in the custodial trust property, or a person interested in the welfare of the beneficiary may petition the court for an accounting by the custodial trustee or the custodial trustee's legal representative.

(c)   A successor custodial trustee may petition the court for an accounting by a predecessor custodial trustee or the legal representative of a predecessor custodial trustee.

(d)   In an action or proceeding under this act or in any other proceeding, the court may require or permit the custodial trustee or the custodial trustee's legal representative to account. The custodial trustee or the custodial trustee's legal representative may petition the court for approval of annual or final accounts.

(e)   If a custodial trustee is removed, the court shall require an accounting and order delivery of the custodial trust property and records to the successor custodial trustee and the execution of all instruments required for transfer of the custodial trust property.

(f)   On petition of the custodial trustee or any person who could petition for an accounting, the court, after notice to interested persons, may issue instructions to the custodial trustee or review the propriety of the acts of a custodial trustee or the reasonableness of compensation determined by the custodial trustee or others. (1995, c. 486, s. 1.)

§ 33B-16. Limitations of action against custodial trustee.

(a)   Except as provided in subsections (b) and (c) of this section, a claim for relief against a custodial trustee for accounting or breach of duty is barred as to a beneficiary, a person to whom custodial trust property is to be paid or delivered, or the legal representative of an incapacitated or deceased beneficiary or payee:

(1) Who has received a final account or statement fully disclosing the matter unless an action or proceeding to assert the claim is commenced within two years after receipt of the final account or statement; or

(2) Who has not received a final account or statement fully disclosing the matter unless an action or proceeding to assert the claim is commenced within three years after the termination of the custodial trust.

(b) Except as provided in subsection (c) of this section, a claim for relief to recover from a custodial trustee for fraud, misrepresentation, or concealment is barred unless an action or proceeding to assert the claim is commenced within five years after the termination of the custodial trust.

(c) A claim for relief is not barred by this section if the claimant:

(1) Is a minor, until the earlier of two years after the claimant becomes an adult or dies;

(2) Is an incapacitated adult, until the earliest of two years after (i) the appointment of a guardian of the estate, (ii) the removal of the incapacity, or (iii) the death of the claimant; or

(3) Was an adult, now deceased, who was not incapacitated, until two years after the claimant's death if the claim was not barred by adjudication, consent, or limitation prior to the claimant's death. (1995, c. 486, s. 1.)

§ 33B-17. Distribution on termination.

(a) Upon termination of a custodial trust, the custodial trustee shall transfer the unexpended custodial trust property:

(1) To the beneficiary, if not incapacitated or deceased;

(2) To the guardian of the estate or other recipient designated by the court for an incapacitated beneficiary; or

(3) Upon the beneficiary's death, in the following order:

a. As last directed in a writing signed by the deceased beneficiary while not incapacitated and received by the custodial trustee during the life of the deceased beneficiary;

b. As designated in the instrument creating the custodial trust; or

c. To the estate of the deceased beneficiary.

(b) If, when the custodial trust would otherwise terminate, the distributee is incapacitated, the custodial trust continues for the use and benefit of the distributee as beneficiary until the incapacity is removed or the custodial trust is otherwise terminated.

(c) Death of a beneficiary does not terminate the power of the custodial trustee to discharge obligations of the custodial trustee or beneficiary incurred before the termination of the custodial trust.

(d) The writing described in G.S. 33B-17(a)(3)a. or the instrument described in G.S. 33B-17(a)(3)b. must also be signed by at least two witnesses, neither of whom is the custodial trustee or the distributee of the custodial trust property, and be acknowledged by the beneficiary or transferor before an individual authorized to administer oaths or take acknowledgements. Failure to comply with the witness or acknowledgement requirement shall not affect the validity of the custodial trust during the life of the beneficiary, but shall invalidate only the direction or designation of the distributee on termination of the custodial trust under G.S. 33B-17(a)(3)a. or G.S. 33B-17(a)(3)b., and upon termination of the custodial trust the custodial trustee shall transfer the unexpended custodial trust property according to the remaining provisions of this section. (1995, c. 486, s. 1.)

§ 33B-18. Methods and forms of creating custodial trusts.

(a) If a transaction (including a declaration with respect to or a transfer of specific property) otherwise satisfies applicable law, the criteria of G.S. 33B-2 are satisfied by:

(1) The execution and either delivery to the custodial trustee or recording of an instrument in substantially the following form:

"TRANSFER UNDER THE NORTH CAROLINA

UNIFORM CUSTODIAL TRUST ACT

I, _____(name of transferor or name and representative capacity if a fiduciary), transfer to _____ (name of trustee other than transferor), as custodial trustee for _____ (name of beneficiary) as beneficiary and _____ as distributee on termination of the trust in absence of direction by the beneficiary under the North Carolina Uniform Custodial Trust Act, the following:

(insert a description of the custodial trust property legally sufficient to identify and transfer each item of property).

Dated: _____

_____ (Seal)   _____
(Witness)

Signature

_____ (Witness)

STATE OF _____ COUNTY OF _____

On this _____ day of_____, ____, personally appeared before me, the said named _____ to me known and known to me to be the person described in and who executed the foregoing instrument and he (or she) acknowledged that he (or she) executed the same and being duly sworn by me, made oath that the statements in the foregoing instrument are true.

My Commission Expires _____

_____

(Signature of Notary Public)

Notary Public (Official Seal)";

or

(2)   The execution and the recording or giving notice of its execution to the beneficiary of an instrument in substantially the following form:

"DECLARATION OF TRUST UNDER THE NORTH CAROLINA

UNIFORM CUSTODIAL TRUST ACT

I, _____(name of owner of property,) declare that henceforth I hold as custodial trustee for _____ (name of beneficiary other than transferor) as beneficiary and _____ as distributee on termination of the trust in absence of direction by the beneficiary under the North Carolina Uniform Custodial Trust Act, the following: (Insert a description of the custodial trust property legally sufficient to identify and transfer each item of property).

Dated: _____

_____ (Seal)   _____
(Witness)

Signature

_____ (Witness)

STATE OF _____ COUNTY OF _____

On this _____ day of_____, ____, personally appeared before me, the said named _____ to me known and known to me to be the person described in and who executed the foregoing instrument and he (or she) acknowledged that he (or she) executed the same and being duly sworn by me, made oath that the statements in the foregoing instrument are true.

My Commission Expires _____

_____

(Signature of Notary Public)

Notary Public (Official Seal)"

(b)   Any customary methods of transferring or evidencing ownership of property may be used to create a custodial trust, including, but not limited to, any of the following:

(1)   Registration of a security in the name of a trust company, an adult other than the transferor, or the transferor if the beneficiary is other than the transferor, designated in substance "as custodial trustee for _____ (name of beneficiary) under the North Carolina Uniform Custodial Trust Act";

(2)   Delivery of a certificated security, or a document necessary for the transfer of an uncertificated security, together with any necessary endorsement, to an adult other than the transferor or to a trust company as custodial trustee, accompanied by an instrument in substantially the form prescribed in subsection (a)(1);

(3)   Payment of money or transfer of a security held in the name of a broker or a financial institution or its nominee to a broker or financial institution for credit to an account in the name of a trust company, an adult other than the transferor, or the transferor if the beneficiary is other than the transferor, designated in substance "as custodial trustee for _____ (name of beneficiary) under the North Carolina Uniform Custodial Trust Act";

(4) Registration of ownership of a life or endowment insurance policy or annuity contract with the issuer in the name of a trust company, an adult other than the transferor, or the transferor if the beneficiary is other than the transferor, designated in substance "as custodial trustee for _____ (name of beneficiary) under the North Carolina Uniform Custodial Trust Act";

(5) Delivery of a written assignment to an adult other than the transferor or to a trust company designated in the assignment in substance by the words "as custodial trustee for _____ (name of beneficiary) under the North Carolina Uniform Custodial Trust Act";

(6) Irrevocable exercise of a power of appointment, pursuant to its terms, in favor of a trust company, an adult other than the donee of the power, or the donee who holds the power if the beneficiary is other than the donee, designated in the appointment in substance "as custodial trustee for _____ (name of beneficiary) under the North Carolina Uniform Custodial Trust Act";

(7) Delivery of a written notification or assignment of a right to future payment under a contract to an obligor which transfers the right under the contract to a trust company, an adult other than the transferor, or the transferor if the beneficiary is other than the transferor, designated in the notification or assignment in substance "as custodial trustee for _____ (name of beneficiary) under the North Carolina Uniform Custodial Trust Act";

(8) Execution and delivery of a conveyance of an interest in real property in the name of a trust company, an adult other than the transferor, or the transferor if the beneficiary is other than the transferor, designated in substance "as custodial trustee for _____ (name of beneficiary) under the North Carolina Uniform Custodial Trust Act";

(9) Issuance of a certificate of title by an agency of a state or of the United States which evidences title to tangible personal property:

a. Issued in the name of a trust company, an adult other than the transferor, or the transferor if the beneficiary is other than the transferor, designated in substance "as custodial trustee for _____ (name of beneficiary) under the North Carolina Uniform Custodial Trust Act"; or

b. Delivered to a trust company or an adult other than the transferor or endorsed by the transferor to that person, designated in substance "as custodial trustee for _____ (name of beneficiary) under the North Carolina Uniform Custodial Trust Act"; or

(10)   Execution and delivery of an instrument of gift to a trust company or an adult other than the transferor, designated in substance "as custodial trustee for _____ (name of beneficiary) under the North Carolina Uniform Custodial Trust Act". (1995, c. 486, s. 1.)

§ 33B-19. Applicable law.

(a)   This act applies to a transfer or declaration creating a custodial trust that refers to this act if, at the time of the transfer or declaration, the transferor, beneficiary, or custodial trustee is a resident of or has its principal place of business in this State or the custodial trust property is located in this State. The custodial trust remains subject to this act despite a later change in residence or principal place of business of the transferor, beneficiary, or custodial trustee, or removal of the custodial trust property from this State.

(b)   A transfer made pursuant to an act of another state substantially similar to this act is governed by the law of that state and may be enforced in this State. (1995, c. 486, s. 1.)

§ 33B-20. Uniformity of application and construction.

This act shall be applied and construed to effectuate its general purpose to make uniform the law with respect to the subject of this act among states enacting it. (1995, c. 486, s. 1.)

§ 33B-21. Short title.

This act may be cited as the "North Carolina Uniform Custodial Trust Act". (1995, c. 486, s. 1.)

§ 33B-22. Limitation on value of custodial trust property.

Transfers or declarations of property to the corpus of a custodial trust under this act shall not exceed in the aggregate one hundred thousand dollars ($100,000) in value, exclusive of the value of the transferor's or declarant's personal residence. This limitation shall not apply to any appreciation in the value of the corpus held in the custodial trust. A good faith violation of this section shall not invalidate a custodial trust. (1995, c. 486, s. 1.)

Vision Books Order Form

Fax Orders:	1-980-299-5965
Phone Orders:	1-704-898-0770
E-mail Orders:	www.visionbooks.org
Mail Orders:	Vision Books, LLC P.O. Box 42406 Charlotte, NC 28215

Shipp To:
Name_____
Address_____
City_____State_____Zip_____
Phone_____Fax_____
Email_____@_____

Bill To: We can bill a third party on your behalf.
Name_____
Address_____
City_____State_____Zip_____
Phone   (   )   Fax_____
Email_____@_____

Pamphlet Number ($15.00 Each)	Qty	Total Cost
_____	_____	_____
_____	_____	_____
_____	_____	_____
_____	_____	_____
_____	_____	_____
_____	_____	_____
_____	_____	_____
_____	_____	_____
<u>Full Volume Set 1-92</u>	<u>92 Pamphlets</u>	<u>1,380.00</u>

Free Shipping Shipping & Handling on Full Volume Orders
Add $1.00 Shipping & Handling per pamphlet $_____

Total Cost $_____

<u>Thank You for Your Support. Management!</u>

DID YOU ENJOY THIS BOOK?

Vision Books would like to hear from you! If you or someone you know has been falsely imprisoned, we would like to hear your story. If the 'North Carolina Criminal Law and Procedure' has had an effect in your life or if you have suggestions, we would like to hear from you. Send your letters to:

Vision Books, LLC
Attn: Staff Writers
P.O. Box 42406
Charlotte, NC 28215
Email: staff@visionbooks.org

Order Additional Copies:

Fax Orders: 1-980-299-5965

Phone Orders: 1-704-898-0770

E-mail Orders: www.visionbooks.org

Mail Orders: Vision Books, LLC
                     P.O. Box 42406
                     Charlotte, NC 28215

www.ingramcontent.com/pod-product-compliance
Lightning Source LLC
Chambersburg PA
CBHW051641170526
45167CB00001B/287